Practice the EIAT!

Practice Questions for the Elevator Industry Aptitude Test

Copyright 2021 Complete Test Preparation Inc. All Rights Reserved.

No part of this book may be reproduced or transferred in any form or by any means, graphic, electronic, or mechanical, including photocopying, recording, web distribution, taping, or by any information storage retrieval system, without the written permission of the author.

Notice: Complete Test Preparation Inc. makes every reasonable effort to obtain from reliable sources accurate, complete, and timely information about the tests covered in this book. Nevertheless, changes can be made in the tests or the administration of the tests at any time and Complete Test Preparation Inc. makes no representation or warranty, either expressed or implied as to the accuracy, timeliness, or completeness of the information contained in this book. Complete Test Preparation Inc. make no representations or warranties of any kind, express or implied, about the completeness, accuracy, reliability, suitability or availability with respect to the information contained in this document for any purpose. Any reliance you place on such information is therefore strictly at your own risk.

The author(s) shall not be liable for any loss incurred as a consequence of the use and application, directly or indirectly, of any information presented in this work. Sold with the understanding, the author is not engaged in rendering professional services or advice. If advice or expert assistance is required, the services of a competent professional should be sought.

The company, product and service names used in this publication are for identification purposes only. All trademarks and registered trademarks are the property of their respective owners. Complete Test Preparation Inc. is not affiliated with any educational institution.

We strongly recommend that students check with exam providers for up-to-date information regarding test content.

Complete Test Preparation Inc. is not affiliated with the makers of the Elevator Industry Aptitude Test, EIAT, who are not involved in the production of, and do not endorse this publication.

ISBN-13: 9781772453393

Version 7.8 April 2021

About Complete Test Preparation Inc.

The Complete Test Preparation Team has been publishing high quality study materials since 2005. Over two million students visit our websites every year, and thousands of students, teachers and parents all over the world (over 100 countries) have purchased our teaching materials, curriculum, study guides and practice tests.

Complete Test Preparation Inc. is committed to providing students with the best study materials and practice tests available on the market. Members of our team combine years of teaching experience, with experienced writers and editors, all with advanced degrees.

Published by
Complete Test Preparation Inc.
Victoria BC Canada

Visit us on the web at https://www.test-preparation.ca
Printed in the USA

Feedback

We welcome your feedback. Email us at feedback@test-preparation.ca with your comments and suggestions. We carefully review all suggestions and often incorporate reader suggestions into upcoming versions. As a Print on Demand Publisher, we update our products frequently.

Contents

6 Getting Started
　　The EIAT Study Plan　　7
　　Making a Study Schedule　　9

12 Practice Test Questions Set 1
　　Answer Key　　51

68 Practice Test Questions Set 2
　　Answer Key　　105

119 Practice Test Questions Set 3
　　Answer Key　　162

176 Conclusion

https://www.facebook.com/CompleteTestPreparation/

https://www.youtube.com/user/MrTestPreparation

Getting Started

CONGRATULATIONS! By deciding to take the Elevator Industry Aptitude Test (EIAT), you have taken the first step toward a great future! Of course, there is no point in taking this important examination unless you intend to do your best to earn the highest grade you possibly can. That means getting yourself organized and discovering the best approaches, methods and strategies to master the material. Yes, that will require real effort and dedication, but if you are willing to focus your energy and devote the study time necessary, before you know it you will be opening that letter of acceptance to the school of your dreams.

We know that taking on a new endeavour can be scary, and it is easy to feel unsure of where to begin. That's where we come in. This study guide is designed to help you improve your test-taking skills, show you a few tricks of the trade and increase both your competency and confidence.

The Elevator Industry Aptitude Test

The EIAT test covers three major areas/subjects. The three subjects covered are:

Reading Comprehension: You need a good grasp of the English language. You are given a short passage, followed by 3 or 4 questions from the passage.

Mechanical Comprehension: This section assess your knowledge of various mechanical concepts, such as pulleys, gears and levers. Elevator repair is very much a mechanics oriented profession.

Arithmetic Computation: Basic math concepts such as fractions, decimals, and percent will be assessed. You are not permitted to use a calculator.

While we seek to make our guide as comprehensive as possible, note that like all exams, the EIAT might be adjusted at some future point. New material might be added, or content that is no longer relevant or applicable might be removed. It is always a good idea to give the materials you receive when you register to take the EIAT a careful review.

This book is for skill practice only! Some of the questions will be easy and others will be more difficult. Go through the practice questions and try your best - by practicing on a range of difficulty levels, you will be ready for the test!

The EIAT Study Plan

Now that you have made the decision to take the EIAT, it is time to get started. Before you do another thing, you will need to figure out a plan of attack. The very best study tip is to start early! The longer the time period you devote to regular study practice, the more likely you will be to retain the material and access it quickly. If you thought that 1x20 is the same as 2x10, guess what? It really is not, when it comes to study time. Reviewing material for just an hour per day over the course of 20 days is far better than studying for two hours a day for only 10 days. The more often you revisit a particular piece of information, the better you will know it. Not only will your grasp and understanding be better, but your ability to reach into your brain and quickly and efficiently pull out the tidbit you need, will be greatly enhanced as well.

The great Chinese scholar and philosopher Confucius believed that true knowledge could be defined as knowing what you know and what you do not know. The first step in preparing for the EIAT Exam is to assess your strengths and weaknesses. You may already have an idea of what you know and what you do not know, but evaluating yourself using our Self-Assessment modules for each of the three areas, Math, English and Reading Comprehension, will clarify the details.

Making a Study Schedule

To make your study time the most productive, you will need to develop a study plan. The purpose of the plan is to organize all the bits of pieces of information in such a way that you will not feel overwhelmed. Rome was not built in a day, and learning everything you will need to know to pass the EIAT Exam is going to take time, too. Arranging the material you need to learn into manageable chunks is the best way to go. Each study session should make you feel as though you have accomplished your goal, or at least are closer, and your goal is simply to learn what you planned to learn during that particular session. Try to organize the content in such a way that each study session builds on previous ones. That way, you will retain the information, be better able to access it, and review the previous bits and pieces at the same time.

Self-assessment

The Best Study Tip! The very best study tip is to start early! The longer you study regularly, the more you will retain and 'learn' the material. Studying for 1 hour per day for 20 days is far better than studying for 2 hours for 10 days.

What don't you know?

The first step is to assess your strengths and weaknesses.

Exam Component	Rate 1 to 5
Reading Comprehension	
Number Operations	
Fractions	
Decimals	
Percent	
Algebra	
Mechanical Comprehension	

Making a Study Schedule

The key to making a study plan is to divide the material you need to learn into manageable size and learn it, while at the same time reviewing the material that you already know.

Using the table above, any scores of 3 or below, you need to spend time learning, reviewing and practicing this subject area. A score of 4 means you need to review the material, but you don't have to spend time re-learning. A score of 5 and you are OK with just an occasional review before the exam.

A score of 0 or 1 means you really need to work on this area and should allocate the most time and the highest priority. Some students prefer a 5-day plan and others a 10-day plan. It also depends on how much time until the exam.

Here is an example of a 5-day plan based on an example from the table above:

Fractions: 1 Study 1 hour everyday – review on last day
Mechanical Comprehension: 3 Study 1 hour for 2 days then ½ hour a day, then review
Percent: 4 Review every second day
Pulleys and Levers: 2 Study 1 hour on the first day – then ½ hour everyday
Reading Comprehension: 5 Review for ½ hour every other day
Algebra: 5 Review for ½ hour every other day
Decimals: 5 very confident – review a few times.

Using this example, Algebra and Decimals are good, and only need occasional review. Mechanical Comprehension is also good and needs 'some' review. Decimals need a bit of work, Pulleys and Levers need a lot of work and Fractions are very weak and need the majority of time. Based on this, here is a sample study plan:

Day	Subject	Time
Monday		
Study	Fractions	1 hour
Study	Pulleys and Levers	1 hour
	½ **hour break**	
Study	Mechanical Comprehension	1 hour
Review	Decimals	½ hour
Tuesday		
Study	Fractions	1 hour
Study	Pulleys and Levers	½ hour
	½ **hour break**	
Study	Decimals	½ hour
Review	Percent	½ hour
Review	Decimals	½ hour
Wednesday		
Study	Fractions	1 hour
Study	Pulleys and Levers	½ hour
	½ **hour break**	
Study	Mechanical Comprehension	½ hour
Review	Decimals	½ hour
Thursday		
Study	Fractions	½ hour
Study	Pulleys and Levers	½ hour
Review	Mechanical Comprehension	½ hour
	½ **hour break**	
Review	Decimals	½ hour
Review	Percent	½ hour

Friday		
Review	Fractions	½ hour
Review	Pulleys and Levers	½ hour
Review	Mechanical Comprehension	½ hour
	½ hour break	
Review	Percent	½ hour
Review	Decimals	½ hour

More Info on Making a Study Plan

5-day Study Plan

https://www.test-preparation.ca/five-day-study-plan-ready-for-blast-off-day/

Use your Daily Routine to Study

https://www.test-preparation.ca/use-your-daily-routine-to-study/

My Best Test Prep Tip – make a study plan

https://www.test-preparation.ca/make-a-study-plan/

How to Make a Study Plan

https://www.test-preparation.ca/how-to-make-a-study-plan/

Practice Test Questions Set 1

The questions below are not the same as you will find on the EIAT - that would be too easy! And nobody knows what the questions will be and they change all the time. Below are general questions that cover the same subject areas as the EIAT. So, while the format and exact wording of the questions may differ slightly, and change from year to year, if you can answer the questions below, you will have no problem with the EIAT.

For the best results, take these practice test questions as if it were the real exam. Set aside time when you will not be disturbed, and a location that is quiet and free of distractions. Read the instructions carefully, read each question carefully, and answer to the best of your ability.

Use the bubble answer sheets provided. When you have completed the Practice Questions, check your answer against the Answer Key and read the explanation provided.

Do not attempt more than one set of practice test questions in one day. After completing the first practice test, wait two or three days before attempting the second set of questions.

This book is for skill practice only! Some of the questions will be easy and others will be more difficult. Go through the practice questions and try your best - by practicing on a range of difficulty levels, you will be ready for the test!

Reading Comprehension

	A	B	C	D	E		A	B	C	D	E
1	○	○	○	○	○	21	○	○	○	○	○
2	○	○	○	○	○	22	○	○	○	○	○
3	○	○	○	○	○	23	○	○	○	○	○
4	○	○	○	○	○	24	○	○	○	○	○
5	○	○	○	○	○	25	○	○	○	○	○
6	○	○	○	○	○	26	○	○	○	○	○
7	○	○	○	○	○	27	○	○	○	○	○
8	○	○	○	○	○	28	○	○	○	○	○
9	○	○	○	○	○	29	○	○	○	○	○
10	○	○	○	○	○	30	○	○	○	○	○
11	○	○	○	○	○						
12	○	○	○	○	○						
13	○	○	○	○	○						
14	○	○	○	○	○						
15	○	○	○	○	○						
16	○	○	○	○	○						
17	○	○	○	○	○						
18	○	○	○	○	○						
19	○	○	○	○	○						
20	○	○	○	○	○						

MATHEMATICS

	A	B	C	D	E		A	B	C	D	E
1	○	○	○	○	○	21	○	○	○	○	○
2	○	○	○	○	○	22	○	○	○	○	○
3	○	○	○	○	○	23	○	○	○	○	○
4	○	○	○	○	○	24	○	○	○	○	○
5	○	○	○	○	○	25	○	○	○	○	○
6	○	○	○	○	○	26	○	○	○	○	○
7	○	○	○	○	○	27	○	○	○	○	○
8	○	○	○	○	○	28	○	○	○	○	○
9	○	○	○	○	○	29	○	○	○	○	○
10	○	○	○	○	○	30	○	○	○	○	○
11	○	○	○	○	○						
12	○	○	○	○	○						
13	○	○	○	○	○						
14	○	○	○	○	○						
15	○	○	○	○	○						
16	○	○	○	○	○						
17	○	○	○	○	○						
18	○	○	○	○	○						
19	○	○	○	○	○						
20	○	○	○	○	○						

Mechanical Comprehension

	A	B	C	D	E		A	B	C	D	E
1	○	○	○	○	○	21	○	○	○	○	○
2	○	○	○	○	○	22	○	○	○	○	○
3	○	○	○	○	○	23	○	○	○	○	○
4	○	○	○	○	○	24	○	○	○	○	○
5	○	○	○	○	○	25	○	○	○	○	○
6	○	○	○	○	○	26	○	○	○	○	○
7	○	○	○	○	○	27	○	○	○	○	○
8	○	○	○	○	○	28	○	○	○	○	○
9	○	○	○	○	○	29	○	○	○	○	○
10	○	○	○	○	○	30	○	○	○	○	○
11	○	○	○	○	○						
12	○	○	○	○	○						
13	○	○	○	○	○						
14	○	○	○	○	○						
15	○	○	○	○	○						
16	○	○	○	○	○						
17	○	○	○	○	○						
18	○	○	○	○	○						
19	○	○	○	○	○						
20	○	○	○	○	○						

Reading Comprehension

Directions: The following questions are based on several reading passages. Each passage is followed by a series of questions. Read each passage carefully, and then answer the questions based on it. You may reread the passage as often as you wish. When you have finished answering the questions based on one passage, go right onto the next passage. Choose the best answer based on the information given and implied.

Questions 1 – 4 refer to the following passage.

Passage 1 - The Life of Helen Keller

Many people have heard of Helen Keller. She is famous because she was unable to see or hear, but learned to speak and read and went onto attend college and earn a degree. Her life is a very interesting story, one that she developed into an autobiography, which was then adapted into both a stage play and a movie. How did Helen Keller overcome her disabilities to become a famous woman? Read on to find out.
Helen Keller was not born blind and deaf. When she was a small baby, she had a very high fever for several days. As a result of her sudden illness, baby Helen lost her eyesight and her hearing. Because she was so young when she went deaf and blind, Helen Keller never had any recollection of being able to see or hear. Since she could not hear, she could not learn to talk. Since she could not see, it was difficult for her to move around. For the first six years of her life, her world was very still and dark.

Imagine what Helen's childhood must have been like. She could not hear her mother's voice. She could not see the beauty of her parent's farm. She could not recognize who was giving her a hug, or a bath or even where her bedroom was each night. Worse, she could not communicate with her parents in any way. She could not express her feelings or tell them the things she wanted. It must have been a very sad childhood.

When Helen was six years old, her parents hired her a teacher named Anne Sullivan. Anne was a young woman who was almost blind. However, she could hear and she could read Braille, so she was a perfect teacher for young Helen. At first, Anne had a very hard time teaching Helen anything. She described her first impression of Helen as a "wild thing, not a child." Helen did not like Anne at first either. She bit and hit Anne when Anne tried to teach her. However, the two of them eventually came to have a great deal of love and respect.

Anne taught Helen to hear by putting her hands on people's throats. She could feel the sounds people made. In time, Helen learned to feel what people said. Next, Anne taught Helen to read Braille, which is a way that books are written for the blind. Finally, Anne taught Helen to talk. Although Helen did learn to talk, it was hard for anyone but Anne to understand her.

As Helen grew older, she amazed more and more people with her story. She went to college and wrote books about her life. She gave talks to the public, with Anne at her side, translating her words. Today, both Anne Sullivan and Helen Keller are famous women who are respected for their lives' work.

1. Helen Keller could not see and hear and so, what was her biggest problem in childhood?

    a. Inability to communicate

    b. Inability to walk

    c. Inability to play

    d. Inability to eat

2. Helen learned to hear by feeling the vibrations people made when they spoke. What were these vibrations were felt through?

    a. Mouth

    b. Throat

    c. Ears

    d. Lips

3. From the passage, we can infer that Anne Sullivan was a patient teacher. We can infer this because

    a. Helen hit and bit her and Anne remained her teacher.

    b. Anne taught Helen to read only.

    c. Anne was hard of hearing too.

    d. Anne wanted to be a teacher.

4. Helen Keller learned to speak but Anne translated her words when she spoke in public. The reason Helen needed a translator was because

    a. Helen spoke another language.

    b. Helen's words were hard for people to understand.

    c. Helen spoke very quietly.

    d. Helen did not speak but only used sign language.

Questions 5 – 7 refer to the following passage.

Passage 2 - Ways Characters Communicate in Theater

Playwrights give their characters voices in a way that gives depth and added meaning to what happens on stage during their play. There are different types of speech in scripts that allow characters to talk with themselves, with other characters, and even with the audience.
It is very unique to theater that characters may talk "to themselves." When characters do this, the speech they give is called a soliloquy. Soliloquies are usually poetic, introspective, moving, and can tell audience members about the feelings, motivations, or suspicions of an individual character without that character having to reveal them to other characters on stage. "To be or not to be" is a famous soliloquy given by Hamlet as he considers difficult but important themes, such as life and death.

The most common type of communication in plays is when one character is speaking to another or a group of other characters. This is generally called dialogue, but can also be called monologue if one character speaks without being interrupted for a long time. It is not necessarily the most important type of communication, but it is the most common because the plot of the play cannot really progress without it. Lastly, and most unique to theater (although it has been used somewhat in film) is when a character speaks directly to the audience. This is called an aside, and scripts usually specifically direct actors to do this. Asides are usually comical, an inside joke between the character and the audience, and very short. The actor will usually face the audience when delivering them, even if it's for a moment, so the audience can recognize this move as an aside.

All three of these types of communication are important to the art of theater, and have been perfected by famous playwrights like Shakespeare. Understanding these types of communication can help an audience member grasp what is artful about the script and action of a play.

5. According to the passage, characters in plays communicate to

    a. move the plot forward

    b. show the private thoughts and feelings of one character

    c. make the audience laugh

    d. add beauty and artistry to the play

6. When Hamlet delivers "To be or not to be," he can be described as

    a. solitary

    b. thoughtful

    c. dramatic

    d. hopeless

7. The author uses parentheses to punctuate "although it has been used somewhat in film,"

    a. to show that films are less important

    b. instead of using commas so that the sentence is not interrupted

    c. because parenthesis help separate details that are not as important

    d. to show that films are not as artistic

Questions 8 – 11 refer to the following passage.

Passage 3 - Low Blood Sugar

As the name suggest, low blood sugar is low sugar levels in the bloodstream. This can occur when you have not eaten properly and undertake strenuous activity, or, when you are very hungry. When Low blood sugar occurs regularly and is ongoing, it is a medical condition called hypoglycemia. This condition can occur in diabetics and in healthy adults.

Causes of low blood sugar can include excessive alcohol consumption, metabolic problems, stomach surgery, pancreas, liver or kidneys problems, as well as a side-effect of some medications.

Symptoms

There are different symptoms depending on the severity of the case.

Mild hypoglycemia can lead to feelings of nausea and hunger. The patient may also feel nervous, jittery and have fast heart beats. Sweaty skin, clammy and cold skin are likely symptoms.
Moderate hypoglycemia can result in a short temper, confusion, nervousness, fear and blurring of vision. The patient may feel weak and unsteady.

Severe cases of hypoglycaemia can lead to seizures, coma,

fainting spells, nightmares, headaches, excessive sweats and severe tiredness.

Diagnosis of low blood sugar

A doctor can diagnosis this medical condition by asking the patient questions and testing blood and urine samples. Home testing kits are available for patients to monitor blood sugar levels. It is important to see a qualified doctor though. The doctor can administer tests to ensure that will safely rule out other medical conditions that could affect blood sugar levels.

Treatment

Quick treatments include drinking or eating foods and drinks with high sugar contents. Good examples include soda, fruit juice, hard candy and raisins. Glucose energy tablets can also help. Doctors may also recommend medications and well as changes in diet and exercise routine to treat chronic low blood sugar.

8. Based on the article, which of the following is true?

    a. Low blood sugar can happen to anyone.

    b. Low blood sugar only happens to diabetics.

    c. Low blood sugar can occur even.

    d. None of the statements are true.

9. Which of the following are the author's opinion?

    a. Quick treatments include drinking or eating foods and drinks with high sugar contents.

    b. None of the statements are opinions.

    c. This condition can occur in diabetics and in healthy adults.

    d. There are different symptoms depending on the severity of the case

10. What is the author's purpose?

    a. To inform

    b. To persuade

    c. To entertain

    d. To analyze

11. Which of the following is not a detail?

    a. A doctor can diagnosis this medical condition by asking the patient questions and testing.

    b. A doctor will test blood and urine samples.

    c. Glucose energy tablets can also help.

    d. Home test kits monitor blood sugar levels.

Questions 12 – 15 refer to the following passage.

How To Get A Good Nights Sleep

Sleep is just as essential for healthy living as water, air and food. Sleep allows the body to rest and replenish depleted energy levels. Sometimes we may for various reasons have trouble sleeping which has a serious effect on our health. Those who have prolonged sleeping problems are facing a serious medical condition and should see a qualified doctor when possible for help. Here is simple guide that can help you sleep better at night.

Try to create a natural pattern of waking up and sleeping around the same time every day. This means avoiding going to bed too early and oversleeping past your usual wake up time. Going to bed and getting up at radically different times everyday confuses your body clock. Try to establish a natural rhythm as much as you can.

Exercises and a bit of physical activity can help you sleep better at night. If you are having problem sleeping, try to be as active as you can during the day. If you are tired from physical activity, falling asleep is a natural and easy process for your body. If you remain inactive during the day, you will find it harder to sleep properly at night. Try walking, jogging, swimming or simple stretches as you get close to your bed time.

Afternoon naps are great to refresh you during the day, but they may also keep you awake at night. If you feel sleepy during the day, get up, take a walk and get busy to keep from sleeping. Stretching is a good way to increase blood flow to the brain and keep you alert so that you don't sleep during the day. This will help you sleep better night.

> A warm bath or a glass of milk in the evening can help your body relax and prepare for sleep. A cold bath will wake you up and keep you up for several hours. Also avoid eating too late before bed.

12. How would you describe this sentence?

    a. A recommendation

    b. An opinion

    c. A fact

    d. A diagnosis

13. Which of the following is an alternative title for this article?

    a. Exercise and a good night's sleep

    b. Benefits of a good night's sleep

    c. Tips for a good night's sleep

    d. Lack of sleep is a serious medical condition

14. Which of the following cannot be inferred from this article?

    a. Biking is helpful for getting a good night's sleep
    b. Mental activity is helpful for getting a good night's sleep
    c. Eating bedtime snacks is not recommended
    d. Getting up at the same time is helpful for a good night's sleep

15. What is a disadvantage of taking naps?

    a. They may keep you awake.
    b. There are no disadvantages
    c. They may help you sleep better
    d. They may affect your diet

Questions 16 – 19 refer to the following passage.

Passage 5 - Pearl Harbor

A Day That Will Live in Infamy! Attack on Pearl Harbor
In 1941, the world was at war. The United States was trying to stay out of the conflict. In Europe, the countries of Germany and Italy had formed an alliance to expand their land and territory. Germany had already taken over Poland, Denmark, and parts of France. They were heading next toward England and due to all the fighting in Europe, there were battles taking place as far south as North Africa, where the German and Italian armies were fighting the British.

This got even worse when the Asian nation of Japan formed an alliance with Germany and Italy. Together, the three countries called themselves, the AXIS. Now, the war was in the Pacific as well as in Europe and Northern Africa. Many Americans felt that perhaps now was the time for the United States to join with its ally, Great Britain and stop the Axis from taking over more regions of the world.

In 1941, Franklin Roosevelt was President of the United States. His fear at the time was that Japan would try to take over many countries in Asia. He did not want to see that happen, so he moved some of the United States warships that had been stationed in San Diego, to the military base at Pearl Harbor, in Honolulu, Hawaii.

Japan quietly plotted their attack. They waited until the early hours of the morning on Sunday, December 7, 1941. Then, 350 Japanese war plans began to drop bombs on the U.S. ships at Pearl Harbor. The first bombs fell at 7:48 am and a mere 90 minutes later, the attack was over. Pearl Harbor was decimated. 8 battleships were damaged. Eleven ships were sunk and 300 U.S. planes were destroyed. Most devastating was the loss of life 2,400 U.S. military members was killed in the attack and 1, 282 were injured.

President Roosevelt addressed the country via the radio and said "Today is a day that will live in infamy." He asked Congress to declare war on Japan. War was declared on Japan on December 8th and on Germany and Italy on December 11th. The United States had entered World War Two.

16. After reading the passage, what can you infer infamy means?

    a. Famous

    b. Remembered in a good way

    c. Remembered in a bad way

    d. Easily forgotten

17. What three countries formed the Axis?

    a. Italy, England, Germany

    b. United States, England, Italy

    c. Germany, Japan, Italy

    d. Germany, Japan, United States

18. What do you think was President Roosevelt's reason for moving warships to Pearl Harbor?

    a. He feared Japan would bomb San Diego

    b. He knew Japan was going to attack Pearl Harbor

    c. He was planning to attack Japan

    d. He wanted to try to protect Asian countries from Japanese takeover

19. Why do you think Japan chose a Sunday morning at 7:48 am for their attack?

    a. They knew the military slept late

    b. There is a law against bombing countries on a Sunday

    c. They wanted the attack to catch people by surprise

    d. That was the only free time they had to attack.

Questions 20 - 23 refer to the following recipe.

If You Have Allergies, You're Not Alone

People who experience allergies might joke that their immune systems have let them down or are seriously lacking. Truthfully though, people who experience allergic reactions or allergy symptoms during certain times of the year have heightened immune systems that are, "better" than those of people who have perfectly healthy but less militant immune systems.

Still, when a person has an allergic reaction, they are having an adverse reaction to a substance that is considered normal to most people. Mild allergic reactions usually have symptoms like itching, runny nose, red eyes, or bumps or discoloration of the skin. More serious allergic reactions, such as those to animal and insect poisons or certain foods, may result in the closing of the throat, swelling of the eyes, low blood pressure, inability to breath, and can even be fatal.

Different treatments help different allergies, and which one a person uses depends on the nature and severity of the allergy. It is recommended to patients with severe allergies to take extra precautions, such as carrying an EpiPen, which treats anaphylactic shock and may prevent death, always in order for the remedy to be readily available and more effective. When an allergy is not so severe, treatments may be used just relieve a person of uncomfortable symptoms. Over the counter allergy medicines treat milder symptoms, and can be bought at any grocery store and used in moderation to help people with allergies live normally.

There are many tests available to assess whether a person has allergies or what they may be allergic to, and advances in these tests and the medicine used to treat patients continues to improve. Despite this fact, allergies still affect many people throughout the year or even every day. Medicines used to treat allergies have side-effects, and it is difficult to bring the body into balance with the use of medicine. Regardless, many of those who live with allergies are grateful for what is available and find it useful in maintaining their lifestyles.

20. According to this passage, which group does the word "militant" belong in

   a. sickly, ailing, faint

   b. strength, power, vigor

   c. active, fighting, warring

   d. worn, tired, breaking down

21. The author says that "medicines used to treat allergies have side-effects of their own" to

   a. point out that doctors aren't very good at diagnosing and treating allergies

   b. argue that because of the large number of people with allergies, a cure will never be found

   c. explain that allergy medicines aren't cures and some compromise must be made

   d. argue that more wholesome remedies should be researched and medicines banned

22. It can be inferred that _____ recommend that some people with allergies carry medicine with them.

    a. the author
    b. doctors
    c. the makers of EpiPen
    d. people with allergies

23. **The author has written this passage to**

    a. inform readers on symptoms of allergies so people with allergies can get help
    b. persuade readers to be proud of having allergies
    c. inform readers on different remedies so people with allergies receive the right help
    d. describe different types of allergies, their symptoms, and their remedies

Questions 24 – 25 refer to the following email.

SUBJECT: MEDICAL STAFF CHANGES

To all staff:

This email is to advise you of a paper on recommended medical staff changes has been posted to the Human Resources website.

The contents are of primary interest to medical staff, other staff may be interested in reading it, particularly those in medical support roles.

The paper deals with several major issues:

    1. Improving our ability to attract top quality staff to the hospital, and retain our existing staff. These changes will make our position and departmental names internationally recognizable and comparable with North American and North Asian departments and positions.

2. Improving our ability to attract top quality staff by introducing greater flexibility in the departmental structure.

3. General comments on issues to be further discussed relative to research staff.

The changes outlined in this paper are significant. I encourage you to read the document and send to me any comments you may have, so that it can be enhanced and improved.

Gordon Simms
Administrator,
Seven Oaks Regional Hospital

24. Are all hospital staff required to read the document posted to the Human Resources website?

    a. Yes all staff are required to read the document.

    b. No, reading the document is optional.

    c. Only medical staff are required to read the document.

    d. none of the above are correct.

25. Have the changes to medical staff been made?

    a. Yes, the changes have been made.

    b. No, the changes are only being discussed.

    c. Some of the changes have been made.

    d. None of the choices are correct.

Questions 26 – 29 refer to the following passage.

When a Poet Longs to Mourn, He Writes an Elegy

Poems are an expressive, especially emotional, form of writing. They have been in literature virtually from the time civilizations invented the written word. Poets often portrayed as moody, secluded, and even troubled, but this is because poets are introspective and feel deeply about the current events and cultural norms they are surrounded with. Poets often produce the most telling literature, giving insight into the society and mind-set they come from. This can be done in many forms.

The oldest types of poems often include many stanzas, may or may not rhyme, and are more about telling a story than experimenting with language or words. The most common types of ancient poetry are epics, which are usually extremely long stories that follow a hero through his journey, or ellegies, which are often solemn in tone and used to mourn or lament something or someone. The Mesopotamians are often said to have invented the written word, and their literature is among the oldest in the world, including the epic poem titled "Epic of Gilgamesh." Similar in style and length to "Gilgamesh" is "Beowulf," an ellegy written in Old English and set in Scandinavia. These poems are often used by professors as the earliest examples of literature.

The importance of poetry was revived in the Renaissance. At this time, Europeans discovered the style and beauty of ancient Greek arts, and poetry was among those. Shakespeare is the most well-known poet of the time, and he used poetry not only to write poems but also to write plays for the theater. The most popular forms of poetry during the Renaissance included villanelles, (a nineteen-line poetic form) sonnets, as well as the epic. Poets during this time focused on style and form, and developed very specific rules and outlines for how an exceptional poem should be written.

As often happens in the arts, modern poets have rejected the constricting rules of Renaissance poets, and free form poems are much more popular. Some modern poems would read just like stories if they weren't arranged into lines and stanzas. It is difficult to tell which poems and poets will be the most important, because works of art often become more famous in hindsight, after the poet has died and society can look at itself without being in the moment. Modern poetry continues to develop, and will no doubt continue to change as values, thought, and writing continue to change.

Poems can be among the most enlightening and uplifting

texts for a person to read if they are looking to connect with the past, connect with other people, or try to gain an understanding of what is happening in their time.

26. In summary, the author has written this passage

   a. as a foreword that will introduce a poem in a book or magazine

   b. because she loves poetry and wants more people to like it

   c. to give a brief history of poems

   d. to convince students to write poems

27. The author organizes the paragraphs mainly by

   a. moving chronologically, explaining which types of poetry were common in that time

   b. talking about new types of poems each paragraph and explaining them a little

   c. focusing on one poet or group of people and the poems they wrote

   d. explaining older types of poetry so she can talk about modern poetry

28. The author's claim that poetry has been around "virtually from the time civilizations invented the written word" is supported by the detail that

   a. Beowulf is written in Old English, which is not really in use any longer

   b. epic poems told stories about heroes

   c. the Renaissance poets tried to copy Greek poets

   d. the Mesopotamians are credited with both inventing the word and writing "Epic of Gilgamesh"

29. According to the passage, the word "telling" means

    a. speaking

    b. significant

    c. soothing

    d. wordy

Questions 30 refers to the following passage.

Scottish Wind Farms

The Scottish Government has a targeted plan of generating 100% of Scotland's electricity through renewable energy by 2020. Renewable energy sources include sun, water and wind power. Scotland uses all forms but its fastest growing energy is wind energy. Wind power is generated by wind turbines, placed onshore and offshore. Wind turbines that are grouped together in large numbers are called wind farms. A majority of Scottish citizens say that the wind farms are necessary to meet current and future energy needs, and would like to see an increase in the number of wind farms.

They cite the fact that wind energy does not cause pollution, there are low operational costs, and most importantly, by definition, renewable energy it cannot be depleted.

30. What is Scotland's fastest growing source of renewable energy?

    a. Solar Panels

    b. Hydroelectric

    c. Wind

    d. Fossil Fuels

MATHEMATICS

1. What is 1/3 of 3/4?

    a. 1/4
    b. 1/3
    c. 2/3
    d. 3/4

2. What fraction of $75 is $1500?

    a. 1/14
    b. 3/5
    c. 7/10
    d. 1/20

3. 3.14 + 2.73 + 23.7 =

    a. 28.57
    b. 30.57
    c. 29.56
    d. 29.57

4. A woman spent 15% of her income on an item and ends with $120. What percentage of her income is left?

    a. 12%
    b. 85%
    c. 75%
    d. 95%

5. Express 0.27 + 0.33 as a fraction.

    a. 3/6
    b. 4/7
    c. 3/5
    d. 2/7

6. What is (3.13 + 7.87) X 5?

    a. 65
    b. 50
    c. 45
    d. 55

7. Reduce 2/4 X 3/4 to lowest terms.

    a. 6/12
    b. 3/8
    c. 6/16
    d. 3/4

8. 2/3 – 2/5 =

    a. 4/10
    b. 1/15
    c. 3/7
    d. 4/15

9. 2/7 + 2/3 =

    a. 12/23
    b. 5/10
    c. 20/21
    d. 6/21

10. 2/3 of 60 + 1/5 of 75 =

    a. 45
    b. 55
    c. 15
    d. 50

11. 8 is what percent of 40?

    a. 10%
    b. 15%
    c. 20%
    d. 25%

12. 9 is what percent of 36?

    a. 10%
    b. 15%
    c. 20%
    d. 25%

13. Three tenths of 90 equals:

    a. 18
    b. 45
    c. 27
    d. 36

14. .4% of 36 is

    a. 1.44
    b. .144
    c. 14.4
    d. 144

15. What is the difference between 700,653 and 70,099?

   a. 4,607,854
   b. 5,460
   c. 700,765
   d. 630,554

16. Simplify 0.12 + 1 2/5 – 1 3/5

   a. 1 1/25
   b. 3 3/25
   c. 1 2/5
   d. 2 3/5

17. Simplify 0.25 + 1/3 + 2/3

   a. 1 1/4
   b. 2 1/4
   c. 1 1/3
   d. 2 1/4

18. Brad has agreed to buy everyone a Coke. Each drink costs $1.89, and there are 5 friends. Estimate Brad's cost.

   a. $7
   b. $8
   c. $10
   d. $12

19. Calculate (14 + 2) x 2 + 3

   a. 21
   b. 35
   c. 80
   d. 43

20. Solve 3/4 + 2/4 + 1.2

   a. 1 1/7
   b. 2 3/4
   c. 2 9/20
   d. 3 1/4

21. John earns $550 a month. He spends 72% of his income and the rest of it goes into his savings account. How much money does he save every year?

   a. $154
   b. $396
   c. $1848
   d. $4752

22. Convert 3 3/8 to decimal correct to 3 decimal places:

   a. 3.375
   b. 0.375
   c. 0.038
   d. 33.750

23. A car salesman receives a 20% commission on the sale of each car. He sold an Audi and his commission was $8,840. What was the price of the car?

   a. $ 88,400
   b. $ 44.200
   c. $ 53,040
   d. $ 35,36

24. Sarah spends 35% of her monthly salary on a dress. If her monthly salary is $135, what is the cost of the dress?

   a. $35
   b. $47.25
   c. $60.30
   d. $87

25. Hannah bought 3 notebooks, 3 pencils and 3 erasers. 19 The price of one pencil is 1/8th of the price of the notebook. One eraser cost $0.5 more than the pencil. If the total cost of all the items is $91.5, what is the price of one notebook?

   a. $24
   b. $52
   c. $72
   d. $80

26 What is the value of fraction 17/3 in decimal, correct to 2 decimal places?

   a. 5.66
   b. 5.67
   c. 5.6
   d. 5.7

27. Convert 19.2 to fraction.

   a. 96/5
   b. 48/25
   c. 2/19
   d. 19/2

28. Convert 14% to fraction:

    a. 7/50
    b. 1/4
    c. 14/50
    d. 1/14

29. What is (1/8) + (4/7) in decimal, correct to one decimal place?

    a. 0.8
    b. 0.81
    c. 0.812
    d. 0.813

30. Solve (1/3) + 4.2 − 3?

    a. 4/3
    b. 16/19
    c. 27/11
    d. 23/15

Mechanical Comprehension

1. What is mechanical advantage?

    a. The ratio of energy input to energy output, typically where the input is less than the output.

    b. The ratio of energy input to energy output, typically where the input is greater than the output.

    c. The ratio of energy resistance to energy output, typically where the resistance is less than the output.

    d. None of the above

2. **What is the ratio of mechanical advantage of a simple pulley?**

   a. 2:1
   b. 1:1
   c. 3:1
   d. 1:2

3. **Consider moving an object with a lever and a fulcrum. What is the relationship between the distance from the fulcrum and the speed the object will move?**

   a. The farther away from the fulcrum, the faster the object will move.
   b. The closer to the fulcrum, the faster an object will move.
   c. An object will move the fastest when directly above the fulcrum.
   d. None of the above.

4. **Which of the following are examples of a wedge?**

   a. Corkscrew
   b. Scissors
   c. Wheelbarrow
   d. Pulley

5. **Which of the following illustrates the principal of the lever?**

   a. The greater the distance over which the force is applied, the greater the force required (to lift the load).
   b. The greater the distance over which the force is applied, the smaller the force required (to lift the load).
   c. The smaller the distance over which the force is applied, the smaller the force required (to lift the load).
   d. None of the above

6. Consider two gears on separate shafts that mesh. The input gear has 30 teeth and turns at 100 rpm. If the output gear has 40 teeth, how fast is the output gear turning?

   a. 300 rpm
   b. 250 rpm
   c. 75 rpm
   d. 100 rpm

7. Consider two gears on separate shafts that mesh. The input gear has 100 teeth and turns at 50 rpm. If the output gear has 20 teeth, how fast is the output gear turning?

   a. 300 rpm
   b. 250 rpm
   c. 200 rpm
   d. 100 rpm

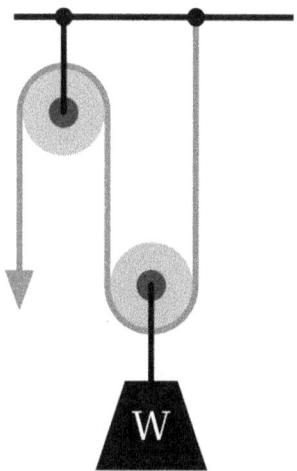

8. Consider the pulley arrangement above. If the weight is 100 pounds, how much force is required to lift it?

   a. 20 pounds
   b. 33 pounds
   c. 50 pounds
   d. 75 pounds

9. Tension of 40 kg. is applied to two springs in parallel, which expands the springs 8 inches. If the same force is applied to springs in series, how far will the springs expand?

   a. 2 inches
   b. 4 inches
   c. 8 inches
   d. 16 inches

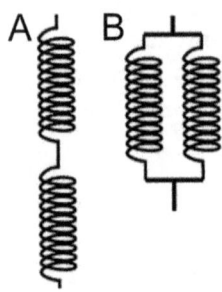

10. Consider the diagram above and select the correct labels from the options below.

   a. A - series, B - parallel
   b. A - parallel, B - series
   c. Series and parallel do not apply to springs
   d. None of the above

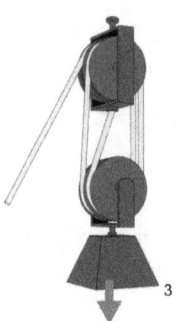

11. Consider the pulley arrangement above. If the weight is 200 pounds, how much force must be exerted downward on the rope?

    a. 200 pounds
    b. 100 pounds
    c. 50 pounds
    d. 25 pounds

12. Up-and-down or back-and-forth motion is called:

    a. Rotary motion
    b. Reciprocating motion
    c. Agitation motion
    d. Harmonic motion

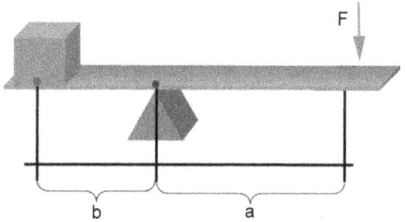

13. Consider the illustration above and the corresponding data:
Weight = W = 80 pounds
Distance from fulcrum to Weight = b = 10 feet
Distance from fulcrum to point where force is applied = a = 20 feet
How much force (F) must be applied to lift the weight?

    a. 80
    b. 40
    c. 20
    d. 10

14. The output torque of a 2 gear train is 1,000 newton-meters, and the gear ratio is 2:1. What is the input force?

   a. 200
   b. 400
   c. 500
   d. 1000

15. Which of the following is an example of torque?

   a. The wheel of a pulley turning
   b. A piston moving
   c. A horse pulling a load
   d. A tow truck pulling a vehicle

16.

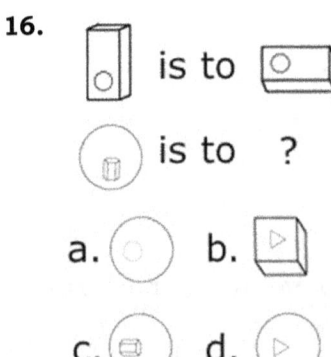

17.

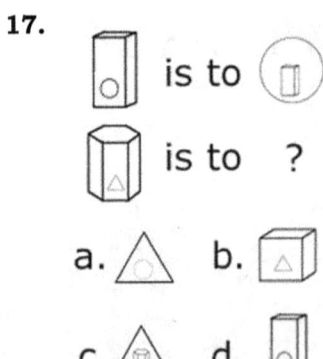

18.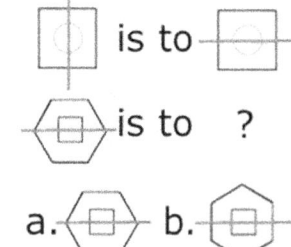

19.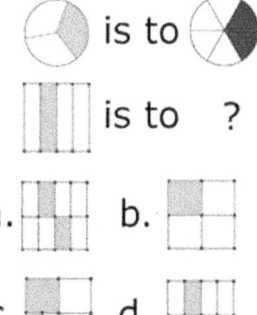

20.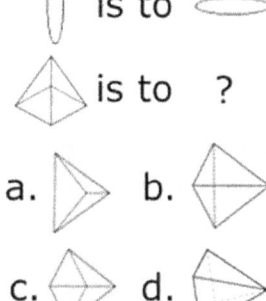

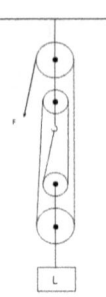

21. Find the weight of the load L in N, if the pulling force F = 20 N.

   a. 5
   b. 100
   c., 20
   d. 80

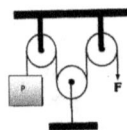

22. Which equation below shows the relationship between F and P for the system of pulleys shown?

   a. P = 3F
   b. P = 2F
   c. P = F
   d. P = F/2

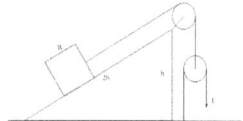

23. How many newtons of force is needed to pull the object up an inclined plane, if the weight of the object is 200 N?

    a. 50
    b. 100
    c. 150
    d. 200

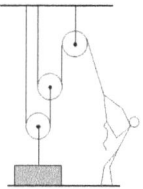

24. How many meters of rope must the boy pull, if he must lift the load 120 cm above the floor?

    a. 4.8
    b. 2.4
    c. 0.6
    d. 0.3

25. How many turns does the gear A make if the gear B makes 100 turns?

   a. 175
   b. 70
   c. 7
   d. 5

26. Which figure represents the assembly of the following pieces?

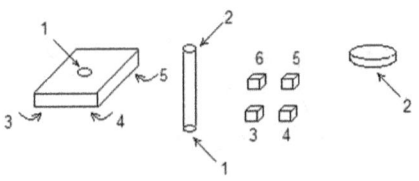

27. When the two longest sides touch what will the shape be?

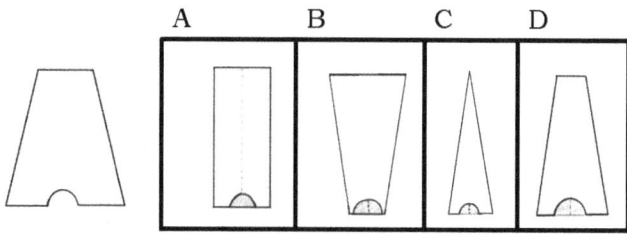

28. When folded, what pattern is possible?

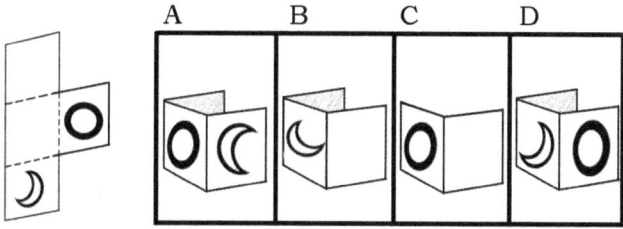

29. When folded into a loop, what will the strip of paper look like?

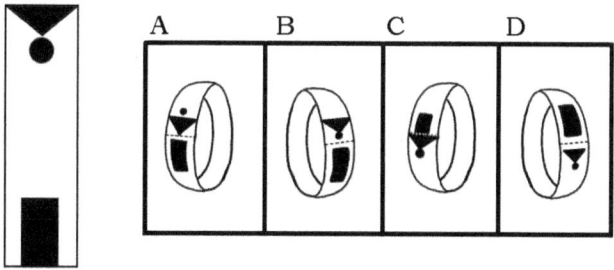

30. Which of the choices is the same pattern at a different angle?

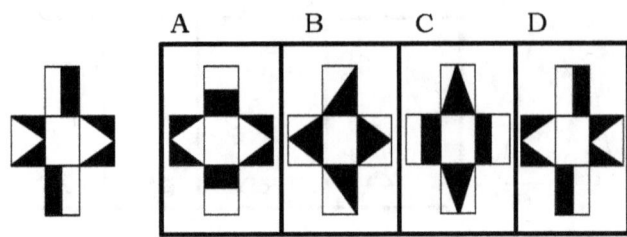

ANSWER KEY

READING COMPREHENSION

1. A
Helen's parents hired Anne to teach Helen to communicate. Choice B is incorrect because the passage states Anne had trouble finding her way around, which means she could walk. Choice C is incorrect because you don't hire a teacher to teach someone to play. Choice D is incorrect because by age 6, if Helen had never eaten, she would have starved to death.

2. B
The correct answer because that fact is stated directly in the passage. The passage explains that Anne taught Helen to hear by allowing her to feel the vibrations in her throat.

3. A
We can infer that Anne is a patient teacher because she did not leave or lose her temper when Helen bit or hit her; she just kept trying to teach Helen. Choice B is incorrect because Anne taught Helen to read and talk. Choice C is incorrect because Anne could hear. She was partially blind, not deaf. Choice D is incorrect because it does not have to do with patience.

4. B
The passage states that it was hard for anyone but Anne to understand Helen when she spoke. Choice A is incorrect because the passage does not mention Helen spoke a foreign language. Choice C is incorrect because there is no mention of how quiet or loud Helen's voice was. Choice D is incorrect because we know from reading the passage that Helen did learn to speak.

5. D
This question tests the reader's summarization skills. The question is asking very generally about the message of the

passage, and the title, "Ways Characters Communicate in Theater," is one indication of that. The other choices A, B, and C are all directly from the text, and therefore readers may be inclined to select one of them, but are too specific to encapsulate the entirety of the passage and its message.

6. B
The paragraph on soliloquies mentions "To be or not to be," and it is from the context of that paragraph that readers may understand that because "To be or not to be" is a soliloquy, Hamlet will be introspective, or thoughtful, while delivering it. It is true that actors deliver soliloquies alone, and may be "solitary" (choice A), but "thoughtful" (choice B) is more true to the overall idea of the paragraph. Readers may choose C because drama and theater can be used interchangeably and the passage mentions that soliloquies are unique to theater (and therefore drama), but this answer is not specific enough to the paragraph in question. Readers may pick up on the theme of life and death and Hamlet's true intentions and select that he is "hopeless" (choice D), but those themes are not discussed either by this paragraph or passage, as a close textual reading and analysis confirms.

7. C
This question tests the reader's grammatical skills. Choice B seems logical, but parenthesis are actually considered to be a stronger break in a sentence than commas are, and along this line of thinking, actually disrupt the sentence more.

Choices A and D make comparisons between theater and film that are simply not made in the passage, and may or may not be true. This detail does clarify the statement that asides are most unique to theater by adding that it is not completely unique to theater, which may have been why the author didn't chose not to delete it and instead used parentheses to designate the detail's importance (choice C).

8. A
Low blood sugar occurs both in diabetics and healthy adults.

9. B
None of the statements are the author's opinion.

10. A
The author's purpose is the inform.

11. A
The only statement that is not a detail is, "A doctor can diagnosis this medical condition by asking the patient questions and testing."

12. A
This sentence is a recommendation.

13. C
Tips for a good night's sleep is the best alternative title for this article.

14. B
Mental activity is helpful for a good night's sleep is can not be inferred from this article.

15. A
From the passage, one disadvantage of taking naps is they may keep you awake at night.

16. C
To be infamous means to be remembered for an evil or terrible action. Therefore, the word infamy means to remember a bad or terrible thing. Choice A is incorrect because being famous is not the same as being infamous. Choice B is incorrect because the attack on Pearl Harbor was not good. Choice D is incorrect because Pearl Harbor was not forgotten.

17. C
Each other answer set contains the name of at least one country that was not part of the AXIS powers.

18. D
It is stated in the passage. Choice A is not correct because there was no indication that Japan would attack San Diego Choice B is incorrect because the attack on Pearl Harbor was a surprise. Choice C is incorrect because Roosevelt was not planning to attack Japan.

19. C
The passage clearly states that Japan planned a surprise attack. They chose that early time to catch the U.S. military off guard. Choice A is incorrect because the military does not sleep late. Choice B is incorrect because there is no law against bombing countries. Choice D is incorrect because it makes no sense.

20. C
This question tests the reader's vocabulary skills. The uses of the negatives "but" and "less," especially right next to each other, may confuse readers into answering with choices A or D, which list words that are antonyms to "militant." Readers may also be confused by the comparison of healthy people with what is being described as an overly healthy person-- both people are good, but the reader may look for which one is "worse" in the comparison, and therefore stray toward the antonym words. One key to understanding the meaning of "militant" if the reader is unfamiliar with it is to look at the root of the word; readers can then easily associate it with "military" and gain a sense of what the word signifies: defence (especially considered that the immune system defends the body). Choice C is correct over choice B because "militant" is an adjective, just as the words in choice C are, whereas the words in choice B are nouns.

21. C
This question tests the reader's understanding of function within writing. The other choices are details included surrounding the quoted text, and may therefore confuse the reader. Choice A somewhat contradicts what is said earlier in the paragraph, which is that tests and treatments are improving, and probably doctors are along with them, but the paragraph doesn't actually mention doctors, and the subject of the question is the medicine. Choice B may seem correct to readers who aren't careful to understand that, while the author does mention the large number of people affected, the author is touching on the realities of living with allergies, rather than the likelihood of curing all allergies. Similarly, while the author does mention the "balance" of the body, which is easily associated with "wholesome," the author is not really making an argument and especially is not making an extreme statement that allergy medicines should be

outlawed. Again, because the article's tone is on living with allergies, choice C is an appropriate choice that fits with the title and content of the text.

22. B
This question tests the reader's inference skills. The text does not state who is doing the recommending, but the use of the "patients," as well as the general context of the passage, lends itself to the logical partner, "doctors," choice B. The author does mention the recommendation but doesn't present it as her own (i.e. "I recommend that"), so choice A may be eliminated. It may seem plausible that people with allergies (choice D) may recommend medicines or products to other people with allergies, but the text does not necessarily support this interaction taking place. Choice C may be selected because the EpiPen is specifically mentioned, but the use of the phrase "such as" when it is introduced is not limiting enough to assume the recommendation is coming from its creators.

23. D
This question tests the reader's global understanding of the text. Choice D includes the main topics of the three body paragraphs, and isn't too focused on a specific aspect or quote from the text, as the other questions are, giving a skewed summary of what the author intended. The reader may be drawn to choice B because of the title of the passage and the use of words like "better," but the message of the passage is larger and more general than this.

24. B
Reading the document posted to the Human Resources website is optional.

25. B
The document is recommended changes and have not be implemented yet.

26. C
This question tests the reader's summarization skills. The use of the word "actually" in describing what kind of people poets are, as well as other moments like this, may lead readers to selecting choices B or D, but the author is more

information than trying to persuade readers. The author gives no indication that she loves poetry (choice B) or that people, students specifically (D), should write poems. Choice A is incorrect because the style and content of this paragraph do not match those of a foreword; forewords usually focus on the history or ideas of a specific poem to introduce it more fully and help it stand out against other poems. The author here focuses on several poems and gives broad statements. Instead, she tells a kind of story about poems, giving three very broad time periods in which to discuss them, thereby giving a brief history of poetry, as choice C states.

27. A
This question tests the reader's summarization skills. Key words in the topic sentences of each of the paragraphs ("oldest," "Renaissance," "modern") should give the reader an idea that the author is moving chronologically. The opening and closing sentence-paragraphs are broad and talk generally. B seems reasonable, but epic poems are mentioned in two paragraphs, eliminating the idea that only new types of poems are used in each paragraph. Choice C is also easily eliminated because the author clearly mentions several different poets, groups of people, and poems. Choice D also seems reasonable, considering that the author does move from older forms of poetry to newer forms, but use of "so (that)" makes this statement false, for the author gives no indication that she is rushing (the paragraphs are about the same size) or that she prefers modern poetry.

28. D
This question tests the reader's attention to detail. The key word is "invented"-- it ties together the Mesopotamians, who invented the written word, and the fact that they, as the inventors, also invented and used poetry. The other selections focus on other details mentioned in the passage, such as that the Renaissance's admiration of the Greeks (choice C) and that Beowulf is in Old English (choice A). Choice B may seem like an attractive answer because it is unlike the others and because the idea of heroes seems rooted in ancient and early civilizations.

29. B
This question tests the reader's vocabulary and contextual-

ization skills. "Telling" is not an unusual word, but it may be used here in a way that is not familiar to readers, as an adjective rather than a verb in gerund form. A may seem like the obvious answer to a reader looking for a verb to match the use they are familiar with. If the reader understands that the word is being used as an adjective and that choice A is a ploy, they may opt to select choice D, "wordy," but it does not make sense in context. Choice C can be easily eliminated, and doesn't have any connection to the paragraph or passage. "Significant" (choice B) makes sense contextually, especially relative to the phrase "give insight" used later in the sentence.

30. C
Wind is the highest source of renewable energy in Scotland. The other choices are either not mentioned at all or not mentioned in the context for how fast they are growing.

MATHEMATICS

1. A
1/3 X 3/4 = 3/12 = 1/4

2. D
75/1500 = 15/300 = 3/60 = 1/20

3. D
3.14 + 2.73 = 5.87 and 5.87 + 23.7 = 29.57

4. B
She spent 15% so, 100% - 15% = 85%

5. C
To convert a decimal to a fraction, take the places of decimal as your denominator, here, 2, so in 0.27, '7' is in the 100th place, so the fraction is 27/100 and 0.33 becomes 33/100.

Next estimate the answer quickly to eliminate obvious wrong choices. 27/100 is about 1/4 and 33/100 is 1/3. 1/3 is slightly larger than 1/4, and 1/4 + 1/4 is 1/2, so the answer will be slightly larger than 1/2.

Looking at the choices, Choice A can be eliminated since 3/6 = 1/2. Choice D, 2/7 is less than 1/2 and can be eliminated. so the answer is going to be Choice B or Choice C.
Do the calculation, 0.27 + 0.33 = 0.60 and 0.60 = 60/100 = 3/5, Choice C is correct.

6. D
3.13 + 7.87 = 11 and 11 X 5 = 55

7. B
2/4 X 3/4 = 6/16, and reduced to the lowest terms = 3/8

8. D
2/3-2/5 = 10-6 /15 = 4/15

9. C
2/7 + 2/3 = 6+14 /21 (21 is the common denominator) = 20/21

10. B
2/3 x 60 = 40 and 1.5 x 75 = 15, 40 + 15 = 55

11. C
This is an easy question, and shows how you can solve some questions without doing the calculations. The question is, 8 is what percent of 40. Take easy percentages for an approximate answer and see what you get.

10% is easy to calculate because you can drop the zero, or move the decimal point. 10% of 40 = 4, and 8 = 2 X 4, so, 8 must be 2 X 10% = 20%.

Here are the calculations which confirm the quick approximation.
8/40 = X/100 = 8 * 100 / 40X = 800/40 = X = 20

12. D
This is the same type of question which illustrates another method to solve quickly without doing the calculations. The question is, 9 is what percent of 36?

Ask, what is the relationship between 9 and 36? 9 X 4 = 36 so they are related by a factor of 4. If 9 is related to 36 by a factor of 4, then what is related to 100 (to get a percent) by a factor of 4?

To visualize:

9 X 4 = 36
Z X 4 = 100

So the answer is 25. 9 has the same relation to 36 as 25 has to 100.

Here are the calculations which confirm the quick approximation.
9/36 = X/100 = 9 * 100 / 36X = 900/36 = 25

13. C
3/10 * 90 = 3 * 90/10 = 27

14. B
4/100 * 36 = .4 * 36/100 = .144

15. D
700,653 − 70,099 = 630,0554

16. B
0.12 + 2/5 + 3/5, Convert decimal to fraction to get 3/25 + (1 2/5 = 7/5 = 35/25) + (1 3/5 = 8/5 = 40/25), = (3 + 35 + 40)/25, = 78/25 = 3 3/25

17. A
0.25 + 2 1/3 + 2/3, first convert decimal to fraction, 1/4 + 1/3 + 2/3, (3 + 4 + 8)/12, = 15/12 = 5/4 = 1 1/4

18. C
If there are 5 friends and each drink costs $1.89, we can round up to $2 per drink and estimate the total cost at, 5 X $2 = $10.
The actual cost is 5 X $1.89 = $9.45.

19. B
(14 + 2) x 2 + 3 = 35. Order or operations, do brackets first, then multiplication and division, then addition and subtraction.

20. C
3/4 + 2/4 + 1.2, first convert the decimal to fraction, = 3/4 + 2/4 + 1 1/5 = ¾ + 2/4 + 6/5 = (find common denominator) (15 + 10 + 24)/20 = 49/20 = 2 9/20

21. C
John spends 72% of his income, which means that he saves 28%. Subtract 72% form total 100% and you get 28%. Now find out what sum of money is 28% of $550.

Step 1: Convert the percentage to decimal. Simple divide it by 100:
28% = 28/100 = 0.28

Step 2: Multiple this by $550
28% of 550 = (28/100)×550 = 0.28 × 550 = 154
Now we know that 28% of $550 is $154 but choice A is not the answer. Why? Because we are asked about the saving of the whole year. $154 is monthly saving. Multiply it by 12 and get the amount saved yearly: 154 x 12 = $1848

22. A
Convert the mixed number to improper fraction (improper fractions have a numerator greater than the denominator).

Numerator = (8 x 3) + 3 = 27
Denominator = 8
Fraction = 27/8
27/8 = 3.375

23. B
Let the total price of the car be equal to 'a'

We are given, 20% of 'a' is equal to $8840.

So,

(20/100) × a = 8840

a = (8840 x 100)/20

a = $44200

Therefore, the price of the car is $44,200

PRACTICE TEST QUESTIONS SET 1

24. B

Percentage spent on dress = (Cost of dress ÷ Total salary)× 100%

Let the Cost of dress be equal to C.

Now,

35% = (C/ 135) × 100%

(35/100) = C/135

Rearranging and making C the subject:

C = (135× 35)/100

C = $47.25

25. A
Let the price of one notebook be equal to 'a'.
Price of one pencil = 1/8 of a = (1/8) × a = 0.125a ....
(1/8 = 0.125)

Price of one eraser = price of pencil + $0.5 = 0.125a + 0.5

Total cost = price of 3 notebooks+ price of 3 pencils + price of 3 erasers

Total cost = 3a + 3(0.125a) + 3(0.125a + 0.5)

3a + 0.375a + 0.375a + 1.5 = 91.5

3.75a + 1.5 = 91.5

3.75a = 91.5 − 1.5

3.75a = 90

a = 90/3.75 = 24

26. B
Divide 17 by 3
17÷3 = 5.6666666667
Answer must be correct to two decimal places. This means that after decimal point there must be 2 digits only.
Answer = 5.67

Remember that while rounding off, the second digit after the decimal is increased by one because the third digit is greater than five.

27. A
To convert any decimal to fraction divide it by a power of 10 and remove the decimal point. The number of digits after decimal determine the power of 10.
Here, 19.2 has one digit after decimal so it will be divided by 10^1
19.2 = 192/10 = 96/5

28. A
To convert percentage to fraction, divide it by 100 and simplify: 14% = 14/100 = 7/50

29. B
Add the fractions:
(1/8) + (4/7) = (7+ 32)/48 = 39/48 = 0.8125

Convert this answer to 2 decimal places
0.81

Notice that the 3rd decimal place is a digit less than five so the second decimal place remains as is.

30. D
Convert the decimal in the equation to fraction before solving.
4.2 = 42/10 = 21/5

(1/3) + (21/5) -3
Lowest Common Multiple of 3 and 5 is 15
(5+63 – 45) / 15
23/15

Mechanical Comprehension

1. A
Mechanical advantage is the ratio of energy input to energy output, typically where the input is less than the output. Mechanical advantage is a measure of the force amplification achieved by using a tool, mechanical device or machine system. Ideally, the device preserves the input power and simply trades off forces against movement to obtain a desired amplification in the output force. The model for this is the law of the lever. Machine components designed to manage forces and movement in this way are called mechanisms. [20]

2. B
The ratio of mechanical advantage of a simple pulley is 1:1.

3. A
The farther away from the fulcrum, the faster the object will move.

4. B
Examples of wedges include the cutting edge of scissors, knives, screwdrivers, doorstops, nails axes and chisels.

5. B
The greater the distance over which the force is applied, the smaller the force required (to lift the load).

6. C
Call the input gear G_1 and the output gear G_2. Call the speed of G_1, S_1 and the number of teeth T_1. Similarly for G_2, we have S_2 and T_2.
Given data:
$S_1 = 100$
$T_1 = 30$
$S_2 = $ unknown
$T_2 = 40$
We know that $S_1 \times T_1 = S_2 \times T_2$
So, $100 \times 30 = S_2 \times 40$
$S_2 = 3000/40 = 75$ rpm

7. B
Call the input gear G_1 and the output gear G_2. Call the speed of G_1, S_1 and the number of teeth T_1. Similarly for G_2, we have S_2 and T_2.

Given data
S_1 - 50
T_1 = 100
S_2 = unknown
T_2 = 20
We know that $S_1 \times T_1 = S_2 \times T_2$

So, 50 X 100 = S_2 X 20
S_2 = 5000/20 = 250 rpm

8. B
Notice the weight is attached to one end of the rope and to one pulley. The force required to lift a 100 pound weight with this arrangement is 100/3 = 33.

9. A
If the springs in parallel expand 10 inches, then the springs in series will expand twice that amount, or 20 inches.

10. A
The correct labels are, A - series, B - parallel

11. C
50 pounds of force much be exerted downward on the rope to lift the 200 pound weight. Since there are 4 pulleys, each will take 1/4 of the load. 200/4 = 50 pounds.

12. B
Up-and-down or back-and-forth motion is called reciprocal motion.

13. B
To solve for F, Weight X b (distance from fulcrum to weight) = Force X a (distance from fulcrum to point where force is applied)
80 X 10 = F X 20
800/20 = F
F = 40

PRACTICE TEST QUESTIONS SET 1

14. C
If the output force is 1,000 newton-meters, and the gear ration is 2:1, the input force will be 1,000/2 = 500.

15. A
The wheel of a pulley turning is an example of torque. Torque, moment or moment of force, is the tendency of a force to rotate an object around an axis, fulcrum, or pivot. Just as a force is a push or a pull, a torque can be thought of as a twist to an object.

16. C
The first pair contains a box with a circle inside, and the same figure on its side.

17. C
The inside and larger shapes are reversed.

18. D
The relation is the same figure rotated.

19. D
The shaded area is divided in half in the second figure.

20. B
The relation is the same figure rotated to the right.

21. D
The block and tackle system composed by a system of pulleys as shown operates according the following rule:

Pulling Force=Load/(Number of supporting ropes)
Here, the number of supporting ropes is 4. So, we have
20 = Load/4
So, Load = 20 × 4 = 80 N
Do not confuse the number of supporting ropes. The rope, which is being pulled is not counted. Otherwise, you will obtain the wrong answer.

22. C
Here, there are 3 fixed pulleys forming a single system. It is known that fixed pulleys do not provide any gain in force. So, we have P = F

23. A

Here we have the combination of two systems composed of an inclined plane and a moveable pulley.

The equation of the inclined plane is

Load/Force=(Path distance)/Height=Mechanical advantage

So, the mechanical advantage MA of the inclined plane is

MA = 2h/h = 2

The equation of the moveable pulley is
Mechanical advantage= (Load)/(Force)=2

Therefore, the total mechanical advantage is 2 × 2 = 4. This means the force needed to lift the 200 N weight is 200N / 4 = 50N.

24. A

Here, we have a moveable pulley system connected to another moveable pulley system. Since the moveable pulley system provides a mechanical advantage equal at 2 (force is half of the load), the equation becomes, for the total mechanical advantage: MA = 2 × 2 = 4.

As the work done on the load is equal to the work done by the force (remember the law of energy conservation), we have:

Load × Load distance=Force × Force distance

Rearranging, the equation,

Load/Force = (Force distance) / (Load distance) = Mechanical advantage

Substituting the values, (Force distance)/(120 cm) = 4

Force distance = 4 × 120 cm = 480 cm = 4.8 m

25. A
The equation of meshed gears states that the speed of rotation V (in rot/s) is inversely proportional to the number of teeth N. Mathematically,
$V_A/V_B = N_B/N_A$

From the figure, it is obvious that $N_A = 20$ and $N_B = 35$. So, since the time of rotation for both gears is equal, we have

$V_A/100 = 35/20$

$V_B = (100 \times 35)/20 = 175$ turns

26. B
If two pieces have the same number at the position shown, it means that point is a junction point. Here, the cylindrical rod is at center of the rectangular platform, the small cubes are below the platform at its edges and the disc is above the rod.

27. D

28. A

29. C

30. B

Practice Test Questions Set 2

The questions below are not the same as you will find on the EIAT - that would be too easy! And nobody knows what the questions will be and they change all the time. Below are general questions that cover the same subject areas as the EIAT. So, while the format and exact wording of the questions may differ slightly, and change from year to year, if you can answer the questions below, you will have no problem with the EIAT.

For the best results, take these practice test questions as if it were the real exam. Set aside time when you will not be disturbed, and a location that is quiet and free of distractions. Read the instructions carefully, read each question carefully, and answer to the best of your ability.

Use the bubble answer sheets provided. When you have completed the Practice Questions, check your answer against the Answer Key and read the explanation provided.

Do not attempt more than one set of practice test questions in one day. After completing the first practice test, wait two or three days before attempting the second set of questions.

This book is for skill practice only! Some of the questions will be easy and others will be more difficult. Go through the practice questions and try your best - by practicing on a range of difficulty levels, you will be ready for the test!

Reading Comprehension

	A	B	C	D	E		A	B	C	D	E
1	○	○	○	○	○	21	○	○	○	○	○
2	○	○	○	○	○	22	○	○	○	○	○
3	○	○	○	○	○	23	○	○	○	○	○
4	○	○	○	○	○	24	○	○	○	○	○
5	○	○	○	○	○	25	○	○	○	○	○
6	○	○	○	○	○	26	○	○	○	○	○
7	○	○	○	○	○	27	○	○	○	○	○
8	○	○	○	○	○	28	○	○	○	○	○
9	○	○	○	○	○	29	○	○	○	○	○
10	○	○	○	○	○	30	○	○	○	○	○
11	○	○	○	○	○						
12	○	○	○	○	○						
13	○	○	○	○	○						
14	○	○	○	○	○						
15	○	○	○	○	○						
16	○	○	○	○	○						
17	○	○	○	○	○						
18	○	○	○	○	○						
19	○	○	○	○	○						
20	○	○	○	○	○						

Mathematics

	A	B	C	D	E		A	B	C	D	E
1	○	○	○	○	○	21	○	○	○	○	○
2	○	○	○	○	○	22	○	○	○	○	○
3	○	○	○	○	○	23	○	○	○	○	○
4	○	○	○	○	○	24	○	○	○	○	○
5	○	○	○	○	○	25	○	○	○	○	○
6	○	○	○	○	○	26	○	○	○	○	○
7	○	○	○	○	○	27	○	○	○	○	○
8	○	○	○	○	○	28	○	○	○	○	○
9	○	○	○	○	○	29	○	○	○	○	○
10	○	○	○	○	○	30	○	○	○	○	○
11	○	○	○	○	○						
12	○	○	○	○	○						
13	○	○	○	○	○						
14	○	○	○	○	○						
15	○	○	○	○	○						
16	○	○	○	○	○						
17	○	○	○	○	○						
18	○	○	○	○	○						
19	○	○	○	○	○						
20	○	○	○	○	○						

Mechanical Comprehension

	A	B	C	D	E		A	B	C	D	E
1	○	○	○	○	○	21	○	○	○	○	○
2	○	○	○	○	○	22	○	○	○	○	○
3	○	○	○	○	○	23	○	○	○	○	○
4	○	○	○	○	○	24	○	○	○	○	○
5	○	○	○	○	○	25	○	○	○	○	○
6	○	○	○	○	○	26	○	○	○	○	○
7	○	○	○	○	○	27	○	○	○	○	○
8	○	○	○	○	○	28	○	○	○	○	○
9	○	○	○	○	○	29	○	○	○	○	○
10	○	○	○	○	○	30	○	○	○	○	○
11	○	○	○	○	○						
12	○	○	○	○	○						
13	○	○	○	○	○						
14	○	○	○	○	○						
15	○	○	○	○	○						
16	○	○	○	○	○						
17	○	○	○	○	○						
18	○	○	○	○	○						
19	○	○	○	○	○						
20	○	○	○	○	○						

Reading Comprehension

Questions 1 - 4 refer to the following passage.

Passage 1 - The Crusades

In 1095 Pope Urban II proclaimed the First Crusade with the intent and stated goal to restore Christian access to holy places in and around Jerusalem. Over the next 200 years there were 6 major crusades and numerous minor crusades in the fight for control of the "Holy Land." Historians are divided on the real purpose of the Crusades, some believing that it was part of a purely defensive war against Islamic conquest; some see them as part of a long-running conflict at the frontiers of Europe; and others see them as confident, aggressive, papal-led expansion attempts by Western Christendom. The impact of the crusades was profound, and judgment of the Crusaders ranges from laudatory to highly critical. However, all agree that the Crusades and wars waged during those crusades were brutal and often bloody. Several hundred thousand Roman Catholic Christians joined the Crusades, they were Christians from all over Europe.

Europe at the time was under the Feudal System, so while the Crusaders made vows to the Church, they also were beholden to their Feudal Lords. This led to the Crusaders not only fighting the Saracen, the commonly used word for Muslim at the time, but also each other for power and economic gain in the Holy Land. This infighting between the Crusaders is why many historians hold the view that the Crusades were simply a front for Europe to invade the Holy Land for economic gain in the name of the Church. Another factor contributing to this theory is that while the army of crusaders marched towards Jerusalem they pillaged the land as they went. The church and feudal Lords vowing to return the land to its original beauty, and inhabitants, this rarely happened though, as the Lords often kept the land for themselves. A full 800 years after the Crusades, Pope John Paul II expressed his sorrow for the massacre of innocent people and the lasting damage that the Medieval church caused in that area of the World.

1. What is the tone of this article?

   a. Subjective
   b. Objective
   c. Persuasive
   d. None of the Above

2. What can all historians agree on concerning the Crusades?

   a. It achieved great things
   b. It stabilized the Holy Land
   c. It was bloody and brutal
   d. It helped defend Europe from the Byzantine Empire

3. What impact did the feudal system have on the Crusades?

   a. It unified the Crusaders
   b. It helped gather volunteers
   c. It had no effect on the Crusades
   d. It led to infighting, causing more damage than good

4. What does Saracen mean?

   a. Muslim
   b. Christian
   c. Knight
   d. Holy Land

Questions 5 - 8 refer to the following passage.

ABC Electric Warranty

ABC Electric Company warrants that its products are free from defects in material and workmanship. Subject to the conditions and limitations set forth below, ABC Electric will, at its option, either repair or replace any part of its products that prove defective due to improper workmanship or materials.

This limited warranty does not cover any damage to the product from improper installation, accident, abuse, misuse, natural disaster, insufficient or excessive electrical supply, abnormal mechanical or environmental conditions, or any unauthorized disassembly, repair, or modification.

This limited warranty also does not apply to any product on which the original identification information has been altered, or removed, has not been handled or packaged correctly, or has been sold as second-hand.

This limited warranty covers only repair, replacement, refund or credit for defective ABC Electric products, as provided above.

5. I tried to repair my ABC Electric blender, but could not, so can I get it repaired under this warranty?

    a. Yes, the warranty still covers the blender

    b. No, the warranty does not cover the blender

    c. Uncertain. ABC Electric may or may not cover repairs under this warranty

Practice Test Questions Set 2

6. My ABC Electric fan is not working. Will ABC Electric provide a new one or repair this one?

    a. ABC Electric will repair my fan

    b. ABC Electric will replace my fan

    c. ABC Electric could either replace or repair my fan can request either a replacement or a repair.

7. My stove was damaged in a flood. Does this warranty cover my stove?

    a. Yes, it is covered.

    b. No, it is not covered.

    c. It may or may not be covered.

    d. ABC Electric will decide if it is covered

8. Which of the following is an example of improper workmanship?

    a. Missing parts

    b. Defective parts

    c. Scratches on the front

    d. None of the above

Questions 9 – 12 refer to the following passage.

Passage 2 - Women and Advertising

Only in the last few generations have media messages been so widespread and so readily seen, heard, and read by so many people. Advertising is an important part of both selling and buying anything from soap to cereal to jeans. For whatever reason, more consumers are women than are men. Media message are subtle but powerful, and more attention has been paid lately to how these message affect women. Of all the products that women buy, makeup, clothes, and other stylistic or cosmetic products are among the most popular. This means that companies focus their advertising on women, promising them that their product will make her feel, look, or smell better than the next company's product will. This competition has resulted in advertising that is more and more ideal and less and less possible for everyday women. However, because women do look to these ideals and the products they represent as how they can potentially become, many women have developed unhealthy attitudes about themselves when they have failed to become those ideals.

In recent years, more companies have tried to change advertisements to be healthier for women. This includes featuring models of more sizes and addressing a huge outcry against unfair tools such as airbrushing and photo editing. There is debate about what the right balance between real and ideal is, because fashion is also considered art and some changes are made to purposefully elevate fashionable products and signify that they are creative, innovative, and the work of individual people. Artists want their freedom protected as much as women do, and advertising agencies are often caught in the middle.

Some claim that the companies who make these changes are not doing enough. Many people worry that there are still not enough models of different sizes and different ethnicities. Some people claim that companies use this healthier type of advertisement not for the good of women, but because they would like to sell products to the women who are looking for these kinds of messages. This is also a hard balance to find: companies need to make money, and women need to feel respected.
While the focus of this change has been on women, advertising can also affect men, and this change will hopefully be a lesson on media for all consumers.

9. The second paragraph states that advertising focuses on women

    a. to shape what the ideal should be

    b. because women buy makeup

    c. because women are easily persuaded

    d. because of the types of products that women buy

10. According to the passage, fashion artists and female consumers are at odds because

  a. there is a debate going on and disagreement drives people apart

  b. both of them are trying to protect their freedom to do something

  c. artists want to elevate their products above the reach of women

  d. women are creative, innovative, individual people

11. The author uses the phrase "for whatever reason" in this passage to

  a. keep the focus of the paragraph on media messages and not on the differences between men and women

  b. show that the reason for this is unimportant

  c. argue that it is stupid that more women are consumers than men

  d. show that he or she is tired of talking about why media messages are important

12. This passage suggests that

  a. advertising companies are still working on making their messages better

  b. all advertising companies seek to be more approachable for women

  c. women are only buying from companies that respect them

  d. artists could stop producing fashionable products if they feel bullied

Questions 13 - 16 refer to the following passage.

FDR, the Treaty of Versailles, and the Fourteen Points

At the conclusion of World War I, those who had won the war and those who were forced to admit defeat welcomed the end of the war and expected that a peace treaty would be signed. The American president, Franklin D. Roosevelt, played an important part in proposing what the agreements should be and did so through his Fourteen Points.

World War I had begun in 1914 when an Austrian archduke was assassinated, leading to a domino effect that pulled the world's most powerful countries into war on a large scale. The war catalysed the creation and use of deadly weapons that had not previously existed, resulting in a great loss of soldiers on both sides of the fighting. More than 9 million soldiers were killed.

The United States agreed to enter the war right before it ended, and many believed that its decision to become finally involved brought on the end of the war. FDR made it very clear that the U.S. was entering the war for moral reasons and had an agenda focused on world peace. The Fourteen Points were individual goals and ideas (focused on peace, free trade, open communication, and self-reliance) that FDR wanted the power nations to strive for now that the war had ended. He was optimistic and had many ideas about what could be accomplished through, and during the post-war peace. However, FDR's fourteen points were poorly received when he presented them to the leaders of other world powers, many of whom wanted only to help their own countries and to punish the Germans for fueling the war, and they fell by the wayside. World War II was imminent, for Germany lost everything.

Some historians believe that the other leaders who participated in the Treaty of Versailles weren't receptive to the Fourteen Points because World War I was fought almost entirely on European soil, and the United States lost much less than did the other powers. FDR was in a unique position to determine the fate of the war, but doing it on his own terms did not help accomplish his goals. This is only one historical example of how the United State has tried to use its power as an important country, but found itself limited because of geological or ideological factors.

13. The main idea of this passage is that

    a. World War I was unfair because no fighting took place in America

    b. World War II happened because of the Treaty of Versailles

    c. the power the United States has to help other countries also prevents it from helping other countries

    d. Franklin D. Roosevelt was one of the United States' smartest presidents

14. According to the second paragraph, World War I started because

    a. an archduke was assassinated

    b. weapons that were more deadly had been developed

    c. a domino effect of allies agreeing to help each other

    d. the world's most powerful countries were large

15. The author includes the detail that 9 million soldiers were killed

    a. to demonstrate why European leaders were hesitant to accept peace

    b. to show the reader the dangers of deadly weapons

    c. to make the reader think about which countries lost the most soldiers

    d. to demonstrate why World War II was imminent

16. According to this passage, catalysed means

    a. analyzed

    b. sped up

    c. invented

    d. funded

Questions 17 - 20 refer to the following passage.

Chocolate Chip Cookies

3/4 cup sugar
3/4 cup packed brown sugar
1 cup butter, softened
2 large eggs, beaten
1 teaspoon vanilla extract
2 1/4 cups all-purpose flour
1 teaspoon baking soda
3/4 teaspoon salt
2 cups semisweet chocolate chips
If desired, 1 cup chopped pecans, or chopped walnuts.
Preheat oven to 375 degrees.

Mix sugar, brown sugar, butter, vanilla and eggs in a large bowl. Stir in flour, baking soda, and salt. The dough will be very stiff.

Stir in chocolate chips by hand with a sturdy wooden spoon. Add the pecans, or other nuts, if desired. Stir until the chocolate chips and nuts are evenly dispersed.

Drop dough by rounded tablespoonfuls 2 inches apart onto a cookie sheet.

Bake 8 to 10 minutes, or, until light brown. Cookies may look underdone, but they will finish cooking after you take them out of the oven.

17. What is the correct order for adding these ingredients?

    a. Brown sugar, baking soda, chocolate chips
    b. Baking soda, brown sugar, chocolate chips
    c. Chocolate chips, baking soda, brown sugar
    d. Baking soda, chocolate chips, brown sugar

18. What does sturdy mean?

    a. Long
    b. Strong
    c. Short
    d. Wide

19. What does disperse mean?

    a. Scatter
    b. To form a ball
    c. To stir
    d. To beat

20. When can you stop stirring the nuts?

    a. When the cookies are cooked.
    b. When the nuts are evenly distributed.
    c. When the nuts are added.
    d. After the chocolate chips are added.

Questions 21 - 23 refer to the following passage.

Lowest Price Guarantee

Get it for less. Guaranteed!

ABC Electric will beat any advertised price by 10% of the difference.

> 1) If you find a lower advertised price, we will beat it by 10% of the difference.
>
> 2) If you find a lower advertised price within 30 days* of your purchase we will beat it by 10% of the difference.
>
> 3) If our own price is reduced within 30 days* of your purchase, bring in your receipt and we will refund the difference.

*14 days for computers, monitors, printers, laptops, tablets, cellular & wireless devices, home security products, projectors, camcorders, digital cameras, radar detectors, portable DVD players, DJ and pro-audio equipment, and air conditioners.

21. I bought a radar detector 15 days ago and saw an ad for the same model only cheaper. Can I get 10% of the difference refunded?

> a. Yes. Since it is less than 30 days, you can get 10% of the difference refunded.
>
> b. No. Since it is more than 14 days, you cannot get 10% of the difference re-funded.
>
> c. It depends on the cashier.
>
> d. Yes. You can get the difference refunded.

22. I bought a flat-screen TV for $500 10 days ago and found an advertisement for the same TV, at another store, on sale for $400. How much will ABC refund under this guarantee?

    a. $100
    b. $110
    c. $10
    d. $400

23. What is the purpose of this passage?

    a. To inform
    b. To educate
    c. To persuade
    d. To entertain

Questions 24 - 27 refer to the following passage.

Passage 6 - What Is Mardi Gras?

Mardi Gras is fast becoming one of the South's most famous and most celebrated holidays. The word Mardi Gras comes from the French and the literal translation is "Fat Tuesday." The holiday has also been called Shrove Tuesday, due to its associations with Lent. The purpose of Mardi Gras is to celebrate and enjoy before the Lenten season of fasting and repentance begins.

What originated by the French Explorers in New Orleans, Louisiana in the 17th century is now celebrated all over the world. Panama, Italy, Belgium and Brazil all host large scale Mardi Gras celebrations, and many smaller cities and towns celebrate this fun loving Tuesday as well. Usually held in February or early March, Mardi Gras is a day of extravagance, a day for people to eat, drink and be merry, to wear costumes, masks and to dance to jazz music.
The French explorers on the Mississippi River would be in shock today if they saw the opulence of the parades and

floats that grace the New Orleans streets during Mardi Gras these days. Parades in New Orleans are divided by organizations. These are more commonly known as Krewes.

Being a member of a Krewe is quite a task because Krewes are responsible for overseeing the parades. Each Krewe's parade is ruled by a Mardi Gras "King and Queen." The role of the King and Queen is to "bestow" gifts on their adoring fans as the floats ride along the street. They throw doubloons, which is fake money and usually colored green, purple and gold, which are the colors of Mardi Gras. Beads in those color shades are also thrown and cups are thrown as well. Beads are by far the most popular souvenir of any Mardi Gras parade, with each spectator attempting to gather as many as possible.

24. The purpose of Mardi Gras is to

    a. Repent for a month.

    b. Celebrate in extravagant ways.

    c. Be a member of a Krewe.

    d. Explore the Mississippi.

25. From reading the passage we can infer that "Kings and Queens,"

    a. Have to be members of a Krewe.

    b. Have to be French.

    c. Have to know how to speak French.

    d. Have to give away their own money.

26. Which group of people began to hold Mardi Gras celebrations?

    a. Settlers from Italy

    b. Members of Krewes

    c. French explorers

    d. Belgium explorers

27. In the context of the passage, what does spectator mean?

    a. Someone who participates actively

    b. Someone who watches the parade's action

    c. Someone on the parade floats

    d. Someone who does not celebrate Mardi Gras

Questions 28 - 30 refer to the following passage.

Passage 1 - Caterpillars

Butterflies and moths have a three stage life cycle. Caterpillars are the first or laval stage. Caterpillars can be either herbivores, feeding mostly on plants, or carnivores, feeding on other insects. Caterpillars eat continuously. Once they are too big for their body, they shed or molt their skin.

Some caterpillars have symbiotic relationships with other insects. A symbiotic relationship is where different species work together in a way that is either harmful or helpful. Symbiotic relationships are critical to many species and ecosystems.

Some caterpillars and ants have a symbiotic or mutual relationship where both benefit. Ants give some protection, and caterpillars provide the ants with honeydew nectar.

Ants and caterpillars communicate by vibrations through the soil as well as grunting and squeaking. Humans are not able to hear these communications.

28. What do most larvae spend their time doing?

    a. Eating

    b. Sleeping

    c. Communicating with ants.

    d. None of the above

29. Are all caterpillars herbivores?

    a. Yes

    b. No, some eat insects

30. What benefit do larvae get from association with ants?

    a. They do not receive any benefit.
    b. Ants give them protection.
    c. Ants give them food.

    d. Ants give them honeydew secretions.

MATHEMATICS

1. 8327 − 1278 =

    a. 7149
    b. 7209
    c. 6059
    d. 7049

2. 294 X 21 =

    a. 6017
    b. 6174
    c. 6728
    d. 5679

3. 1278 + 4920 =

    a. 6298

    b. 6108

    c. 6198

    d. 6098

4. 285 * 12 =

    a. 3420

    b. 3402

    c. 3024

    d. 2322

5. 4120 – 3216 =

    a. 903

    b. 804

    c. 904

    d. 1904

6. 2417 + 1004 =

    a. 3401

    b. 4321

    c. 3402

    d. 3421

7. 1440 ÷ 12 =

    a. 122

    b. 120

    c. 110

    d. 132

8. 2713 − 1308 =

   a. 1450
   b. 1445
   c. 1405
   d. 1455

9. The sale price of a car is $12,590, which is 20% off the original price. What is the original price?

   a. $14,310.40
   b. $14,990.90
   c. $15,108.00
   d. $15,737.50

10. Express 25% as a fraction.

   a. 1/4
   b. 7/40
   c. 6/25
   d. 8/28

11. 143 * 4 =

   a. 572
   b. 702
   c. 467
   d. 672

12. Express 125% as a decimal.

   a. .125
   b. 12.5
   c. 1.25
   d. 125

13. Solve for x: 30 is 40% of x

   a. 60
   b. 90
   c. 85
   d. 75

14. 12½% of x is equal to 50. Solve for x.

   a. 300
   b. 400
   c. 450
   d. 350

15. Express 24/56 as a reduced common fraction.

   a. 4/9
   b. 4/11
   c. 3/7
   d. 3/8

16. Express 87% as a decimal.

   a. .087
   b. 8.7
   c. .87
   d. 87

17. 60 is 75% of x. Solve for x.

   a. 80
   b. 90
   c. 75
   d. 70

18. 10 x 2 − (7 + 9)

   a. 21
   b. 16
   c. 4
   d. 13

19. 60% of x is 12. Solve for x.

   a. 18
   b. 15
   c. 25
   d. 20

20. Express 71/1000 as a decimal.

   a. .71
   b. .0071
   c. .071
   d. 7.1

21. .33 × .59 =

   a. .1947
   b. 1.947
   c. .0197
   d. .1817

22. .84 ÷ .7 =

   a. .12
   b. 12
   c. .012
   d. 1.2

23. .87 - .48 =

   a. .39
   b. .49
   c. .41
   d. .37

24. Susan wants to buy a leather jacket that costs $545.00 and is on sale for 10% off. What is the approximate cost?

   a. $525
   b. $450
   c. $475
   d. $500

25. 1628 / 4 =

   a. 307
   b. 667
   c. 447
   d. 407

26. 46 * 15 =

   a. 590
   b. 690
   c. 490
   d. 790

27. 5575 + 8791

   a. 14,756
   b. 14,566
   c. 14,466
   d. 14,366

28. 6149 / 143 =

    a. 43
    b. 47
    c. 37
    d. 54

29. Jake is driving down to meet his parents who live 125 miles away in a small town. On the way he stops at a gas station and there he reads a mile-marker that says that the Town is 55 miles away. What is the fraction of the journey completed by Jake when stops for gas?

    a. 14/25
    b. 11/25
    c. 7/18
    d. 5/8

30. A Christmas pie is divided into eight equal portions and the parents eat one portion each. The daughter eats 2/3rd of the remaining pie and the rest is eaten by the son. What fraction of the total pie is eaten by the son?

    a. 1/2
    b. 1/4
    c. 1/3
    d. 1/12

Mechanical Comprehension

1. Which of the following is true of the relationship between screws and threads?

    a. The larger the distance between threads, the easier to turn.

    b. The smaller the distance between threads, the easier to turn.

    c. The smaller the distance between threads, the more difficult to turn.

    d. None of the above

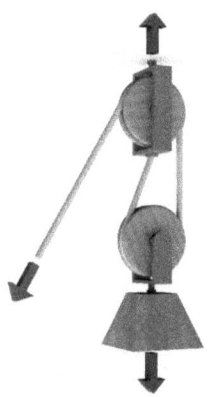

2. Consider the arrangement of pulleys above. If the weight shown is 150 pounds, how much force much be exerted to lift the weight?

    a. 150 pounds

    b. 100 pounds

    c. 75 pounds

    d. 50 pounds

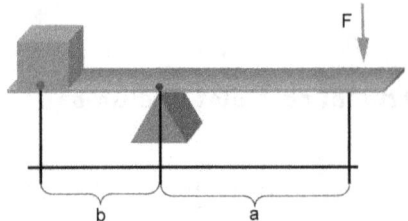

3. Consider the illustration above and the corresponding data:

Weight = W = 100 pounds
Distance from fulcrum to Weight = b = 5 feet
Distance from fulcrum to point where force is applied = a = 10 feet
How much force (F) must be applied to lift the weight?

    a. 100
    b. 50
    c. 25
    d. 10

4. Consider a gear train with 3 gears, from left to right, A with 10 teeth, gear B with 40 teeth, and gear C with 10 teeth. Gear A turns clockwise at 80 rpm. What direction and speed in rpm does Gear C turn?

    a. 100 rpm, clockwise
    b. 80 rpm clockwise
    c. 120 rpm counter clockwise
    d. 100 rpm counter clockwise

5. A force of 40 kg. is applied to two springs in parallel, which compresses the springs 10 inches. If the same force is applied to springs in series, how far will the springs compress?

   a. 40 inches
   b. 20 inches
   c. 10 inches
   d. 5 inches

6. Tension of 40 kg. is applied to two springs in series, which expand the springs 20 inches. If the same amount of tension is applied to springs in parallel, how far will the springs expand?

   a. 20 inches
   b. 10 inches
   c. 5 inches
   d. 2 inch

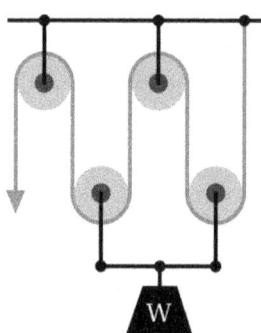

7. Consider the pulley arrangement above. If the weight, W, is 100 pounds, then how much force is required to lift the weight?

   a. 100 pounds
   b. 50 pounds
   c. 25 pounds
   d. 20 pounds

8. A cam is a mechanical linkage that:

a. Transforms linear motion into rotary motion and vice versa.
b. Transforms oscillating motion in to linear motion and vice versa.
c. Transforms reciprocating motion to oscillating motion.
d. None of the above

9. What is the function of the crankshaft?

a. To transform the back-and-forth motion of the pistons into rotary motion.
b. To transform rotary motion into reciprocal motion.
c. To transfer the rotary motion of the cam to the wheels
d. None of the above.

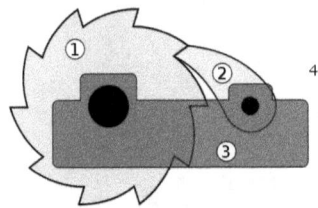

10. Identify the components labelled above.

a. 1 - ratchet, 2 - pawl, 3 - base
b. 1 - pawl, 2 - ratchet, 3 - base
c. 1 - gear, 2 - stop, 3 base
d. None of the above

11. ☐ is to ⌐

◯ is to ?

a.  ⌒ b.  ⌒

c.  ⌒ d.  ⌐

12.  ⬠ is to ⬠

△ is to ?

a.  ▽ b.  ◁

c.  ▷ d.  ⌭

13.  △ is to ▷

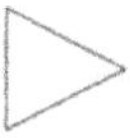

⌭ is to ?

a.  ▷ b. ☐

c. 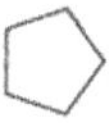 ⬠ d. 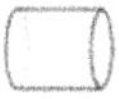 ⌭

14. 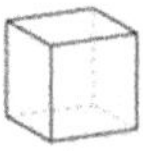 ⬜ is to △

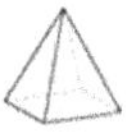

△ is to ?

a.  △ b. ☐

c.  ⬠ d.  ⌭

15.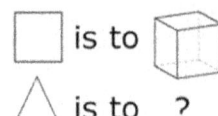

a. △ b. △
c. ⬠ d. ⬭

16. What is the force applied to lift the 400 N weight shown?

   a. 200 N
   b. 300 N
   c. 400 N
   d. 800 N

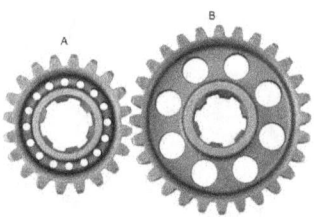

17. How many turns does the gear B make when the gear A makes 14 complete turns?

   a. 8
   b. 10
   c. 20
   d. 28

18. Which of the following is true about the system of meshed gears shown?

    a. Gear A rotates slower than gear B

    b. Gear A rotates slower than gear C

    c. Gear B rotates slower than gear C

    d. Gear B rotates faster than the other two gears

19. Which of the following statements about gears is false?

    a. Gears are teethed wheels used to generate rotation

    b. Meshed gears move at the same time

    c. Meshed gears move at the same speed

    d. Teeth in gears help increase the friction and avoid slipping

20. What direction does the pinion in the figure rotate if the rack shifts on the right?

    a. Clockwise

    b. Counterclockwise

    c. First clockwise then counterclockwise

    d. First counterclockwise, then clockwise

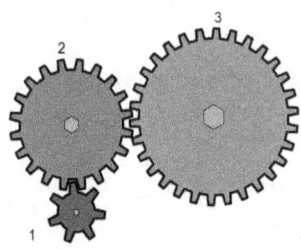

21. How many turns does gear 1 make when gear 3 makes 210 turns?

    a. 30

    b. 90

    c. 300

    d. 900

22. What is the ratio of the load to effort?

   a. Torque
   b. Mechanical Advantage
   c. Energy
   d. Mechanical Energy

23. A door handle is an example of

   a. Inclined plane
   b. Pulley
   c. Screw
   d. Lever

24. In which case below is the work done moving an object against gravity?

   a. When moving the object downwards
   b. When moving the object horizontally
   c. When moving an object upwards
   d. When an object is at rest

25. If there is no friction, the minimum force F needed to move an object at a distance d along a horizontal plane is

   a. Zero
   b. Slightly greater than zero
   c. Equal to the weight of the object
   d. Slightly greater than the weight of the object

26. How many cubes are there in the figure?

 a. 30
 b. 32
 c. 33
 d. 24

27. Which shape must we place on the existing figure to form a perfect square?

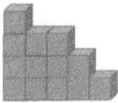

 a.   b.   c.   d.

28. Which shape must we place on the existing figure to form a perfect cube?

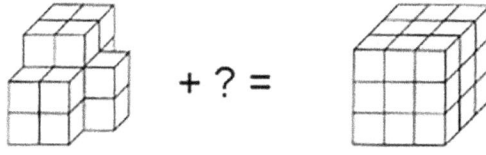

a. 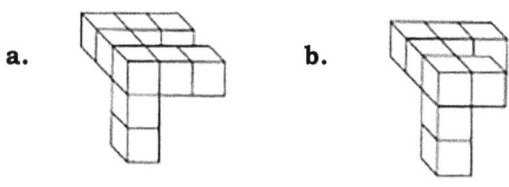 b.

c. d.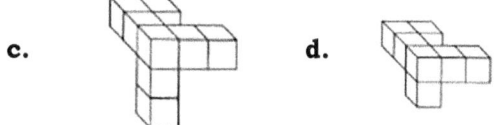

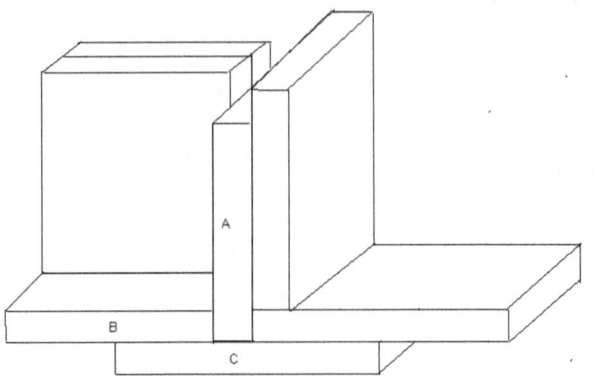

29. How many blocks is the block A in the figure touching?

    a. 7
    b. 6
    c. 5
    d. 4

30. How many blocks is the block B in the figure touching?

    a. 4
    b. 5
    c. 6
    d. 3

Answer Key

1. A
Choice B is incorrect; the author did not express their opinion on the subject matter. Choice C is incorrect, the author was not trying to prove a point, nor is the author trying to persuade.

2. C
Choice C is correct; historians believe it was brutal and bloody. Choice A is incorrect; there is no consensus that the Crusades achieved great things. Choice B is incorrect; it did not stabilize the Holy Lands. Choice D is incorrect, some historians do believe this was the purpose but not all historians.

3. D
The feudal system led to infighting. Choice A is incorrect, it had the opposite effect. Choice B is incorrect, though this is a good answer, it is not the best answer. The Church asked for volunteers not the Feudal Lords. Choice C is incorrect, it did have an effect on the Crusades.

4. A
Saracen was a generic term for Muslims widely used in Europe during the later medieval era.

5. B
This warranty does not cover a product that you have tried to fix yourself. From paragraph two, "This limited warranty does not cover ... any unauthorized disassembly, repair, or modification. "

6. C
ABC Electric could either replace or repair the fan, provided the other conditions are met. ABC Electric has the option to repair or replace.

7. B
The warranty does not cover a stove damaged in a flood. From the passage, "This limited warranty does not cover any damage to the product from improper installation, accident, abuse, misuse, natural disaster, insufficient or excessive electrical supply, abnormal mechanical or environmental conditions."

A flood is an "abnormal environmental condition," and a natural disaster, so it is not covered.

8. A
A missing part is an example of defective workmanship. This is an error made in the manufacturing process. A defective part is not considered workmanship.

9. D
This question tests the reader's summarization skills. The other choices A, B, and C focus on portions of the second paragraph that are too narrow and do not relate to the specific portion of text in question. The complexity of the sentence may mislead students into selecting one of these answers, but rearranging or restating the sentence will lead the reader to the correct answer. In addition, choice A makes an assumption that may or may not be true about the intentions of the company, choice B focuses on one product rather than the idea of the products, and choice C makes an assumption about women that may or may not be true and is not supported by the text.

10. B
This question tests reader's attention to detail. If a reader selects A, he or she may have picked up on the use of the word "debate" and assumed, very logically, that the two are at odds because they are fighting; however, this is simply not supported in the text. Choice C also uses very specific quotes from the text, but it rearranges and gives them false meaning. The artists want to elevate their creations above the creations of other artists, thereby showing that they are "creative" and "innovative." Similarly, choice D takes phrases straight from the text and rearranges and confuses them. The artists are described as wanting to be "creative, innovative, individual people," not the women.

11. A
This question tests reader's vocabulary and summarization skills. This phrase, used by the author, may seem flippant and dismissive if readers focus on the word "whatever" and misinterpret it as a popular, colloquial term. In this way, choices B and C may mislead the reader to selecting one of them by including the terms "unimportant" and "stupid,"

respectively. Choice D is a similar misreading, but doesn't make sense when the phrase is at the beginning of the passage and the entire passage is on media messages. Choice A is literally and contextually appropriate, and the reader can understand that the author would like to keep the introduction focused on the topic the passage is going to discuss.

12. A
This question tests a reader's inference skills. The extreme use of the word "all" in choice B suggests that every single advertising company are working to be approachable, and while this is not only unlikely, the text specifically states that "more" companies have done this, signifying that they have not all participated, even if it's a possibility that they may some day. The use of the limiting word "only" in choice C lends that answer similar problems; women are still buying from companies who do not care about this message, or those companies would not be in business, and the passage specifies that "many" women are worried about media messages, but not all. Readers may find choice D logical, especially if they are looking to make an inference, and while this may be a possibility, the passage does not suggest or discuss this happening. Choice A is correct based on specifically because of the relation between "still working" in the answer and "will hopefully" and the extensive discussion on companies struggles, which come only with progress, in the text.

13. C
This question tests the reader's summarization skills. The entire passage is leading up to the idea that the president of the US may not have had grounds to assert his Fourteen Points when other countries had lost so much. Choice A is pretty directly inferred by the text, but it does not adequately summarize what the entire passage is trying to communicate. Choice B may also be inferred by the passage when it says that the war is "imminent," but it does not represent the entire message, either. The passage does seem to be in praise of FDR, or at least in respect of him, but it does not in any way claim that he is the smartest president, nor does this represent the many other points included. Choice C is then the obvious answer, and most directly relates to the closing sentences which it rewords.

14. C
This question tests the reader's attention to detail. The passage does state that choices A and B are true, and while those statements are in proximity to the explanation for why the war started, they are not the reason given. Choice D is a mix up of words used in the passage, which says that the largest powers were in play but not that this fact somehow started the war. The passage does make a direct statement that a domino effect started the war, supporting choice C as the correct answer.

15. A
This question tests the reader's understanding of functions in writing. Throughout the passage, it states that leaders of other nations were hesitant to accept generous or peaceful terms because of the grievances of the war, and the great loss of life was chief among these. While the passage does touch on the devastation of deadly weapons (B), the use of this raw, emotional fact serves a much larger purpose, and the focus of the passage is not the weapons. While readers may indeed consider who lost the most soldiers (C) when, so many countries were involved and the inequalities of loss are mentioned in the passage, there is no discussion of this in the passage. Choice D is related to A, but choice A is more direct and relates more to the passage.

16. B
This question tests the reader's vocabulary skills. Choice A may seem appealing to readers because it is phonetically similar to "catalysed," but the two are not related in any other way. Choice C makes sense in context, but if plugged in to the sentence creates a redundancy that doesn't make sense. Choice D does also not make sense contextually, even if the reader may consider that funds were needed to create more weaponry, especially if it was advanced.

17. A
The correct order of ingredients is brown sugar, baking soda and chocolate chips.

18. B
Sturdy: strong, solid in structure or person. In context, Stir in chocolate chips by hand with a *sturdy* wooden spoon.

19. A
Disperse: to scatter in different directions or break up. In context, Stir until the chocolate chips and nuts are evenly *dispersed.*

20. B
You can stop stirring the nuts when they are evenly distributed. From the passage, "Stir until the chocolate chips and nuts are evenly dispersed."

21. B
The time limit for radar detectors is 14 days. Since you made the purchase 15 days ago, you do not qualify for the guarantee.

22. B
Since you made the purchase 10 days ago, you are covered by the guarantee. Since it is an advertised price at a different store, ABC Electric will "beat" the price by 10% of the difference, which is,

500 – 400 = 100 – difference in price

100 X 10% = $10 – 10% of the difference

The advertised lower price is $400. ABC will beat this price by 10% so they will refund $100 + 10 = $110.

23. C
The purpose of this passage is to persuade.

24. B
The correct answer can be found in the fourth sentence of the first paragraph.

Choice A is incorrect because repenting begins the day AFTER Mardi Gras. Choice C is incorrect because you can celebrate Mardi Gras without being a member of a Krewe.

Choice D is incorrect because exploration does not play any role in a modern Mardi Gras celebration.

25. A
The second sentence is the last paragraph states that Krewes

are led by the Kings and Queens. Therefore, you must have to be part of a Krewe to be its King or its Queen.

Choice B is incorrect because it never states in the passage that only people from France can be Kings and Queen of Mardi Gras

Choice C is incorrect because the passage says nothing about having to speak French.

Choice D is incorrect because the passage does state that the Kings and Queens throw doubloons, which is fake money.

26. C
The first sentences of BOTH the 2nd and 3rd paragraphs mention that French explorers started this tradition in New Orleans.
Choices A, B and D are incorrect because they are names of cities or countries listed in the 2nd paragraph.

27. B
In the final paragraph, the word spectator is used to describe people who are watching the parade and catching cups, beads and doubloons.

Choices A and C are incorrect because we know the people who participate are part of Krewes. People who work the floats and parades are also part of Krewes

Choice D is incorrect because the passage makes no mention of people who do not celebrate Mardi Gras.

28. A
Caterpillars spend most of their time eating.

29. B
Some caterpillars are herbivores, others eat other insects (carnivores).

30. B
From the passage, the ants provide some degree of protection.

MATHEMATICS

1. D
8327 − 1278 = 7049

2. B
294 X 21 = 6174

3. C
1278 + 4920 = 6198

4. A
285 * 12 = 3420

5. C
4120 − 3216 = 904

6. D
2417 + 1004 = 3421

7. B
1440 ÷ 12 = 120

8. C
2713 − 1308 = 1405

9. D
Original price = x,
80/100 = 12590/X,
80X = 1259000,
X = 15737.50.

10. A
25% = 25/100 = 1/4

11. A
143 * 4 = 572

12. C
125/100 = 1.25

13. D
40/100 = 30/X = 40X = 30*100 = 3000/40 = 75

14. B
12.5/100 = 50/X = 12.5X = 50 * 100 = 5000/12.5 = 400

15. C
24/56 = 3/7 (divide numerator and denominator by 8)

16. C
Converting percent to decimal – divide percent by 100 and remove the % sign. 87% = 87/100 = .87

17. A
60 has the same relation to X as 75 to 100 – so
60/X = 75/100
6000 = 75X
X = 80

18. C
10 x 2 – (7 + 9) = 4

19. D
60 has the same relationship to 100 as 12 does to X – so
60/100 = 12/X
1200 = 60X
X = 20

20. C
Converting a fraction to a decimal – divide the numerator by the denominator – so 71/1000 = .071. Dividing by 1000 moves the decimal point 3 places.

21. A
.33 × .59 = .1947

22. D
.84 ÷ .7 = 1.2

23. A
.87 - .48 = .39

24. D
The jacket costs $545.00 so we can round up to $550. 10% of $550 is 55. We can round down to $50, which is easier to work with. $550 - $50 is $500. The jacket will cost about $500.
The actual cost will be 10% X 545 = $54.50
545 – 54.50 = $490.50

25. D
1628 / 4 = 407

26. B
46 * 15 = 690

27. D
5575 + 8791 = 14,366

28. A
6149 / 143 = 43

29. A
Distance covered by Jake when he stops for gas
= Total distance – Distance left

Let the distance covered by jake when he stops for gas be represented by variable 'a'

a = 125 – 55 = 70 miles
Fraction of distance covered = 70/125
After simplification the fraction is = 14/25

30. B
Carefully read the step and solve step by step:

Step 1: Find the fraction eaten by parents
Pie is divided into eight pieces. Parents eat one portion each. This means the parents ate 2 out of eight portions.

Therefore, the fraction of pie eaten by parents = 2/8 = ¼

Step 2: Subtract that fraction from 1 to find the portion eaten by children
Now that we know the parents ate 1/4th.

Lets find how much is left for children.
Pie left for children = 1- (1/4) = ¾

Step 3: Find the fraction of whole pie eaten by daughter
Now we know that 3/4th of the pie is left for the children. The daughter eats 2/3rd of the pie left.

Note that the fraction mentioned in question the daughter eats is not of the whole pie. This fraction is the fraction with respect to the portion left that is 3/4th of the whole pie.

To find the portion of whole pie eaten by the daughter we find 2/3 of 3/4.

Mathematically,
(2/3) of (3/4) = (2/3) × (3/4) = 1/2
This means that daughter eats 1/2 of the whole pie.

Step 4: Subtract the portion of daughter from the total portion of children to find the fraction eaten by the son:
Fraction eaten by the son = (3/4) – (1/2) = (3-2)/4 = 1/4
Therefore, the fraction of pie eaten by the son is 1/4

MECHANICAL COMPREHENSION

1. B
The smaller the distance between threads, the easier to turn.

2. C
75 pounds of force much be exerted downward on the rope to lift the 150 pound weight.

3. B
To solve for F, Weight X b (distance from fulcrum to weight) = Force X a (distance from fulcrum to point where force is applied)
100 X 5 = F X 10
500/10 = F
F = 50

4. B
First calculate the speed of gear B. The gear ratio is 10:40

or 1:4. If gear A is turning at 80 rpm, then gear B, which is larger, will turn slower, 80/4 = 20 rpm.

Next calculate B and C. Gear C is smaller, so it will turn faster. The gear ratio is 40:10 or 4:1, and since gear B turns at 20 rpm, gear C will turn at 20 X 4 = 80 rpm.

Next calculate the direction. Gear A is turning clockwise, so Gear B is turning counter clockwise, so Gear C must be turning clockwise.

5. B
If the springs in parallel compress 10 inches, then the springs in series will expand half that amount, or 20 inches.

6. B
If the springs in parallel expand 20 inches, then the springs in series will expand twice that amount, or 10 inches.

7. C
Notice the weight is attached to two of the pulleys. The weight required will therefore be 100/4 = 25 pounds.

8. B
A cam is a rotating or sliding piece in a mechanical linkage used especially in transforming rotary motion into linear motion or vice-versa

9. A
The function of the crankshaft is to transform the back-and-forth motion of the pistons into rotary motion.

10. A
The labelled components are, 1 - ratchet, 2 - pawl, 3 - base.

11. C
The second figure is half the first figure.

12. A
The second figures is rotated 180 degrees.

13. D
The relation is an upright figure to a figure rotated to the right.

14. D
The relation is a solid figures to one that is 2-dimentional and has one fewer sides.

15. B
The relation is a 2-dimentional figure to a 3-dimentional figure.

16. A
Here, we have a system of combined pulley, i.e. one fixed and one moveable. The fixed pulley does not provide any mechanical advantage while the moveable pulley provides a mechanical advantage of 2.

So, the force required to lift the 400 N weight (load) is:
F = W/2 = 400N/2 = 200N

17. B
The equation of meshed gears states that the speed of rotation V (in rot/s) is inversely proportional to the number of teeth N. Mathematically,

$V_A/V_B = N_B/N_A$

From the figure, it is obvious that $N_A = 20$ and $N_B = 28$. So, we have

$14/V_B = 28/20$

$V_B = (14 \times 20)/28 = 10$ turns

18. C
In meshed gears, larger the gear, slower the rotation and vice versa. Thus, if you look the figure carefully, you can find that the gear B rotates slower than the others and gear A rotates the fastest.

19. C
Choice A is correct. Gears are teethed wheels used to generate rotation.
Choice B is correct. Meshed gears move at the same time as they are connected.
Choice C is false. Meshed gears move at different speed depending on their size. Larger gears move slower than smaller gears.

Choice D is correct. Teeth in gears help increase the friction and avoid slipping.

20. B
If the rack shifts to the right, the lower part of the pinion moves right as well. This means the entire pinion rotates counterclockwise.

21. D
The equation of meshed gears states that the speed of rotation V (in rot/s) is inversely proportional to the number of teeth N. Mathematically,

$N_1 \cdot V_1 = N_2 \cdot V_2 = N_3 \cdot V_3$
Here, we are concerned only for the gears 1 and 3. Thus, we have
$7 \cdot V_1 = 30 \cdot 210$
$V_1 = (30 \cdot 210)/7 = 900$ turns

22. D
The ratio of the load to the effort is known as Mechanical Advantage (MA). It shows how many times easier it would be to perform an action using the simple machine compared to not using it. Mechanical advantage has no unit.

23. D
The door handle has a turning effect when a force acts on it. Therefore, it is an example of a Lever (first class) as the turning point is between the force and load (they are in the opposite sides of the door).

24. C
Choice A is incorrect. When we move an object downwards, we are acting in the direction of gravity.
Choice B is incorrect. As gravity acts vertically down, the horizontal motion is not affected by it. So, there is no work against the gravity when moving an object horizontally.
Choice C is correct. When lifting an object upwards, we act against the gravity (which acts downwards). As a result, the work done in this case is against the gravity.
Choice D is incorrect. When an object is at rest, there is no work done on it.

25. B
If there is no friction, the object's weight does not affect its horizontal motion. Thus, we need a minimum force (slightly greater than zero) to move it on a horizontal plane a distance d.

26. C
In the bottom row, there are 3 × 4 + 3 = 15 cubes.
In the next row, there are 2 + 3 + 3 + 3 + 1 = 12 cubes.
In the third row, there are 2 + 2 = 4 cubes.
In the upper row, there are only 2 cubes.
Thus, in total there are 15 + 12 + 4 + 2 = 33 cubes.

27. A
The figure has 4 rows and 5 columns, with not all of them are complete. It is obvious that in order to be a perfect square, it must have 5 × 5 dimensions.

From the figure, you may see that the first (bottom) row is complete. In the second row one cube is missing, in the third row two cubes are missing, in the fourth row four cubes are missing and in the fifth row all 5 cubes are missing. There missing cubes must be filled with one of the shapes.

28. A
If you rotate the shapes in the choices by 900 clockwise, you will notice that the missing shape to form a perfect cube is the first one.

29. B
From the figure, block A touches 6 blocks (1 is below, 2 are lateral in vertical position (narrow face), 2 are lateral in the horizontal position and one is lateral in the vertical position (wider side).

30. A
From the figure, block B touches 1 block below, 2 blocks above and one block laterally, i.e. in total 4 blocks.

Practice Test Questions 3

The questions below are not the same as you will find on the EIAT - that would be too easy! And nobody knows what the questions will be and they change all the time. Below are general questions that cover the same subject areas as the EIAT. So, while the format and exact wording of the questions may differ slightly, and change from year to year, if you can answer the questions below, you will have no problem with the EIAT.

For the best results, take these practice test questions as if it were the real exam. Set aside time when you will not be disturbed, and a location that is quiet and free of distractions. Read the instructions carefully, read each question carefully, and answer to the best of your ability.

Use the bubble answer sheets provided. When you have completed the Practice Questions, check your answer against the Answer Key and read the explanation provided.

Do not attempt more than one set of practice test questions in one day. After completing the first practice test, wait two or three days before attempting the second set of questions.

This book is for skill practice only! Some of the questions will be easy and others will be more difficult. Go through the practice questions and try your best - by practicing on a

range of difficulty levels, you will be ready for the test!

READING COMPREHENSION

	A	B	C	D	E		A	B	C	D	E
1	○	○	○	○	○	21	○	○	○	○	○
2	○	○	○	○	○	22	○	○	○	○	○
3	○	○	○	○	○	23	○	○	○	○	○
4	○	○	○	○	○	24	○	○	○	○	○
5	○	○	○	○	○	25	○	○	○	○	○
6	○	○	○	○	○	26	○	○	○	○	○
7	○	○	○	○	○	27	○	○	○	○	○
8	○	○	○	○	○	28	○	○	○	○	○
9	○	○	○	○	○	29	○	○	○	○	○
10	○	○	○	○	○	30	○	○	○	○	○
11	○	○	○	○	○						
12	○	○	○	○	○						
13	○	○	○	○	○						
14	○	○	○	○	○						
15	○	○	○	○	○						
16	○	○	○	○	○						
17	○	○	○	○	○						
18	○	○	○	○	○						
19	○	○	○	○	○						
20	○	○	○	○	○						

Mathematics

	A	B	C	D	E		A	B	C	D	E
1	○	○	○	○	○	21	○	○	○	○	○
2	○	○	○	○	○	22	○	○	○	○	○
3	○	○	○	○	○	23	○	○	○	○	○
4	○	○	○	○	○	24	○	○	○	○	○
5	○	○	○	○	○	25	○	○	○	○	○
6	○	○	○	○	○	26	○	○	○	○	○
7	○	○	○	○	○	27	○	○	○	○	○
8	○	○	○	○	○	28	○	○	○	○	○
9	○	○	○	○	○	29	○	○	○	○	○
10	○	○	○	○	○	30	○	○	○	○	○
11	○	○	○	○	○						
12	○	○	○	○	○						
13	○	○	○	○	○						
14	○	○	○	○	○						
15	○	○	○	○	○						
16	○	○	○	○	○						
17	○	○	○	○	○						
18	○	○	○	○	○						
19	○	○	○	○	○						
20	○	○	○	○	○						

Mechanical Comprehension

	A	B	C	D	E			A	B	C	D	E
1	○	○	○	○	○		21	○	○	○	○	○
2	○	○	○	○	○		22	○	○	○	○	○
3	○	○	○	○	○		23	○	○	○	○	○
4	○	○	○	○	○		24	○	○	○	○	○
5	○	○	○	○	○		25	○	○	○	○	○
6	○	○	○	○	○		26	○	○	○	○	○
7	○	○	○	○	○		27	○	○	○	○	○
8	○	○	○	○	○		28	○	○	○	○	○
9	○	○	○	○	○		29	○	○	○	○	○
10	○	○	○	○	○		30	○	○	○	○	○
11	○	○	○	○	○							
12	○	○	○	○	○							
13	○	○	○	○	○							
14	○	○	○	○	○							
15	○	○	○	○	○							
16	○	○	○	○	○							
17	○	○	○	○	○							
18	○	○	○	○	○							
19	○	○	○	○	○							
20	○	○	○	○	○							

Directions: The following questions are based on several reading passages. Each passage is followed by a series of questions. Read each passage carefully, and then answer the questions based on it. You may reread the passage as often as you wish. When you have finished answering the questions based on one passage, go right onto the next passage. Choose the best answer based on the information given and implied.

Questions 1 – 4 refer to the following passage.

Who Was Anne Frank?

You may have heard mention of the word Holocaust in your History or English classes. The Holocaust took place from 1939-1945. It was an attempt by the Nazi party to purify the human race, by eliminating Jews, Gypsies, Catholics, homosexuals and others they deemed inferior to their "perfect" Aryan race. The Nazis used Concentration Camps, which were sometimes used as Death Camps, to exterminate the people they held in the camps. The saddest fact about the Holocaust was the over one million children under the age of sixteen died in a Nazi concentration camp. Just a few weeks before World War II was over, Anne Frank was one of those children to die.

Before the Nazi party began its persecution of the Jews, Anne Frank had a happy live. She was born in June of 1929. In June of 1942, for her 13th birthday, she was given a simple present which would go onto impact the lives of millions of people around the world. That gift was a small red diary that she called Kitty. This diary was to become Anne's most treasured possession when she and her family hid from the Nazi's in a secret annex above her father's office building in Amsterdam.

For 25 months, Anne, her sister Margot, her parents, another family, and an elderly Jewish dentist hid from the Nazis in this tiny annex. They were never permitted to go outside, and their food and supplies were brought to them by Miep Gies and her husband, who did not believe in the Nazi persecution of the Jews. It was a very difficult life for young Anne and she used Kitty as an outlet to describe her life in hiding. After 2 years, Anne and her family were betrayed and arrested by the Nazis. To this day, nobody is exactly sure who betrayed the Frank family and the other annex residents. Anne, her mother, and her sister were separated from Otto Frank, Anne's father. Then, Anne and Margot were separated from their mother. In March of 1945, Margot Frank died of starvation in a Concentration Camp. A few days later, at the age of 15, Anne Frank died of typhus. Of all the people who hid in the Annex, only Otto Frank survived the Holocaust.

Otto Frank returned to the Annex after World War II. It was there that he found Kitty, filled with Anne's thoughts and feelings about being a persecuted Jewish girl. Otto Frank had Anne's diary published in 1947 and it has remained continuously in print ever since. Today, the diary has been published in over 55 languages and more than 24 million copies have been sold around the world. The Diary of Anne Frank tells the story of a brave young woman who tried to see the good in all people.

1. From the context clues in the passage, what does the word Annex mean?

    a. Attic

    b. Bedroom

    c. Basement

    d. Kitchen

2. Why do you think Anne's diary has been published in 55 languages?

    a. So everyone could understand it.

    b. So people around the world could learn more about the horrors of the Holocaust.

    c. Because Anne was Jewish but hid in Amsterdam and died in Germany.

    d. Because Otto Frank spoke many languages.

3. From the description of Anne and Margot's deaths in the passage, what can we assume typhus is?

  a. The same as starving to death.

  b. An infection the Germans gave to Anne.

  c. A disease Anne caught in the concentration camp.

  d. Poison gas used by the Germans to kill Anne.

4. In the third paragraph, what does the word outlet mean?

  a. A place to plug things into the wall

  b. A store where Miep bought cheap supplies for the Frank family

  c. A hiding space similar to an Annex

  d. A place where Anne could express her private thoughts.

Questions 5 – 8 refer to the following passage.

Was Dr. Seuss A Real Doctor?

A favorite author for over 100 years, Theodor Seuss Geisel was born on March 2, 1902. Today, we celebrate the birthday of the famous "Dr. Seuss" by hosting Read Across America events throughout the March. School children around the country celebrate the "Doctor's" birthday by making hats, giving presentations and holding read aloud circles featuring some of Dr. Seuss' most famous books.

But who was Dr. Seuss? Did he go to medical school? Where was his office? You may be surprised to know that Theodor Seuss Geisel was not a medical doctor at all. He took on the nickname Dr. Seuss when he became a noted children's book author. He earned the nickname because people said his books were "as good as medicine." All these years later, his nickname has lasted and he is known as Dr. Seuss all across the world.

Think back to when you were a young child. Did you ever want to try "green eggs and ham?" Did you try to "Hop on Pop?" Do you remember learning about the environment from a creature called The Lorax? Of course, you must recall one of Seuss' most famous characters; that green Grinch who stole Christmas. These stories were all written by Dr. Seuss and featured his signature rhyming words and letters. They also featured made up words to enhance his rhyme scheme and even though many of his characters were made up, they sure seem real to us today.

And what of his "signature" book, The Cat in the Hat? You must remember that cat and Thing One and Thing Two from your childhood. Did you know that in the early 1950's there was a growing concern in America that children were not becoming avid readers? This was, book publishers thought, because children found books dull and uninteresting. An intelligent publisher sent Dr. Seuss a book of words that he thought all children should learn as young readers. Dr. Seuss wrote his famous story The Cat in the Hat, using those words. We can see, over the decades, just how much influence his writing has had on very young children. That is why we celebrate this doctor's birthday each March.

5. What does the word "avid" mean in the last paragraph?

    a. Good

    b. Interested

    c. Slow

    d. Fast

6. What can we infer from the statement " His books were like medicine?"

    a. His books made people feel better

    b. His books were in doctor's office waiting rooms

    c. His books took away fevers

    d. His books left a funny taste in readers' mouths.

7. Why is the publisher in the last paragraph called "intelligent?"

a. The publisher knew how to read.

b. The publisher knew kids did not like to read.

c. The publisher knew Dr. Seuss would be able to create a book that sold well.

d. The publisher knew that Dr. Seuss would be able to write a book that would get young children interested in reading.

8. The theme of this passage is

a. Dr. Seuss was not a doctor.

b. Dr. Seuss influenced the lives of generations of young children.

c. Dr. Seuss wrote rhyming books.

d. Dr. Seuss' birthday is a good day to read a book.

Questions 9 - 11 refer to the following passage.

Keeping Tropical Fish

Keeping tropical fish at home or in your office used to be very popular. Today, interest has declined, but it remains as rewarding and relaxing a hobby as ever. Ask any tropical fish hobbyist, and you will hear how soothing and relaxing watching colorful fish live their lives in the aquarium. If you are considering keeping tropical fish as pets, here is a list of the basic equipment you will need.

A filter is essential for keeping your aquarium clean and your fish alive and healthy. There are different types and sizes of filters and the right size for you depends on the size of the aquarium and the level of stocking. Generally, you need a filter with a 3 to 5 times turn over rate per hour. This means that the water in the tank should go through the filter about 3 to 5 times per hour.

Most tropical fish do well in water temperatures ranging between 24° C and 26° C, though each has its own ideal water temperature. A heater with a thermostat is necessary to regulate the water temperature. Some heaters are submersible and others are not, so check carefully before you buy.

Lights are also necessary, and come in a large variety of types, strengths and sizes. A light source is necessary for plants in the tank to photo-synthesize and give the tank a more attractive appearance. Even if you plan to use plastic plants, the fish still require light, although here you can use a lower strength light source.

A hood is necessary to keep dust, dirt and unwanted materials out of the tank. Sometimes the hood can also help prevent evaporation. Another requirement is aquarium gravel. This will improve the aesthetics of the aquarium and is necessary if you plan to have real plants.

9. What is the general tone of this article?

    a. Formal

    b. Informal

    c. Technical

    d. Opinion

10. Which of the following cannot be inferred?

    a. Gravel is good for aquarium plants.

    b. Fewer people have aquariums in their office than at home.

    c. The larger the tank, the larger the filter required.

    d. None of the above.

11. What evidence does the author provide to support their claim that aquarium lights are necessary?

a. Plants require light.

b. Fish and plants require light.

c. The author does not provide evidence for this statement.

d. Aquarium lights make the aquarium more attractive.

12. Which of the following is an opinion?

a. Filter with a 3 to 5 times turn over rate per hour are required.

b. Aquarium gravel improves the aesthetics of the aquarium.

c. An aquarium hood keeps dust, dirt and unwanted materials out of the tank.

d. Each type of tropical fish has its own ideal water temperature.

Questions 13 - 15 refer to the following passage.

The Civil War

The Civil War began on April 12, 1861. The first shots of the Civil War were fired in Fort Sumter, South Carolina. Even though more American lives were lost in the Civil War than in any other war, not one person died on that first day. The war began because eleven Southern states seceded from the Union and tried to start their own government, The Confederate States of America.

Why did the states secede? The issue of slavery was a primary cause of the Civil War. The eleven southern states relied heavily on their slaves to foster their farming and plantation lifestyles. The northern states, many of whom had already abolished slavery, did not feel that the southern states should have slaves. The north wanted to free all the slaves and President Lincoln's goal was to both end slavery and preserve the Union. He had Congress declare war on the Confederacy on April 14, 1862. For four long, blood soaked years, the North and South fought.

From 1861 to mid 1863, it seemed as if the South would win this war. However, on July 1, 1863, an epic three day battle was waged on a field in Gettysburg, Pennsylvania. Gettysburg is remembered for being the bloodiest battle in American history. At the end of the three days, the North turned the tide of the war in their favor. The North then went on to dominate the South for the remainder of the war. Another famous event is General Sherman's "March to The Sea," where he famously led the Union Army through Georgia and the Carolinas, burning and destroying everything in their path.

In 1865, the Union army invaded and captured the Confederate capital of Richmond Virginia. Robert E. Lee, leader of the Confederacy surrendered to General Ulysses S. Grant, leader of the Union forces, on April 9, 1865. The Civil War was over and the Union was preserved.

13. What does secede mean?

    a. To break away from

    b. To accomplish

    c. To join

    d. To lose

14. Which of the following statements summarizes a FACT from the passage?

    a. Congress declared war and then the Battle of Fort Sumter began.

    b. Congress declared war after shots were fired at Fort Sumter.

    c. President Lincoln was pro slavery

    d. President Lincoln was at Fort Sumter with Congress

15. Which event finally led the Confederacy to surrender?

    a. The battle of Gettysburg

    b. The battle of Bull Run

    c. The invasion of the confederate capital of Richmond

    d. Sherman's March to the Sea

Questions 16 - 19 refer to the following passage.

Social Media Use in Teens Linked to Poor Sleep, Anxiety.

Source: [By Agata Blaszczak-Boxe, Originally published on Live Science, September 2015]

According to a new study, the pressure to be available 24/7 on social media may lead to poorer sleep quality as well as an increased risk of depression and anxiety in teens. In the study, researchers asked 467 teenagers ages 11 to 17 about their use of social media during the day and at night. In other tests, they examined the teens' sleep quality, self-esteem, anxiety and depression.

They also looked at whether and to what extent the kids felt the pressure to be available on social media all the time. The researchers found that using social media at any point was significantly related to decreased sleep quality, lower self-esteem, and increased depression levels in the study participants. However, when it comes to sleep quality, "those who log on at night appear to be particularly affected," study author Heather Cleland Woods, of the University of Glasgow in Scotland, said in a statement. Research presented at the American Psychological Association meeting in 2011 found a link between the use of social media in teens and traits linked to schizophrenia and depression.

In another study, published this year in the journal Cyber psychology, Behavior, and Social Networking, frequent social media use in teens was tied to an increased risk of poor mental health. "Since adolescence is a vulnerable period for development of long-term issues, it is essential that we understand how adolescents' social media use relates to" factors like sleep quality and the risk of depression, the researchers wrote in the new study. Cleland Woods suggested that families use what she calls a "digital sunset," to minimize the potential negative effects of social media use on sleep and feelings of well-being. "Turn off the devices and the blue light, stop checking emails and social media, and allow yourself time to finish your day," she said. "Sleep is important, so put your phone away. "Still, Cleland Woods stressed that the use of social media itself is not a negative activity. "We all do it," she told Live Science. "However, we need to think about how and when we are online."

16. Which of the following best summarizes author's point of view in the passage?

    a. One major reason of diseases such as anxiety, depression, and schizophrenia is social media.

    b. Day time usage of social media is safer as compared to engagement at night.

    c. Excessive usage of social media in teens has been found to link with deprived sleep and poor mental health.

    d. Young people should avoid use of social media as it can affect their beliefs and cause long term psychological issues.

17. By using the term "digital sunset," Author refers to:

    a. Artificially creating darker surroundings at home

    b. Sleeping before actual sunset

    c. Turning off the Television

    d. Turning off all gadgets which link to internet and social media.

18. Which of the following CANNOT be inferred directly from the passage?

   a. Youth experiences pressure to be available on social media usually, which is causing sleep depravity and anxiety.

   b. Youngsters with online presence at night are more affected, with respect to quality of sleep.

   c. Risk of depression, anxiety and schizophrenia increase with deficiency of sleep.

   d. Social media itself is not the problem. Nevertheless, excessive usage can cause adverse effects.

19. Which of the following specifically describes the word "adolescents" used in the passage?

   a. People under the age of 25
   b. Pubescents
   c. Adults
   d. Children under the age of 12

Questions 20 - 23 refer to the following passage.

Frequent Travelers

Source: [By A.W, Originally published in The Economist, August 2015]

Researchers at the University of Surrey, in Britain, and Linnaeus University, in Sweden, have published a new study highlighting what they call "a darker side of hypermobility." The "hypermobile"—largely but not exclusively business travelers—have won a certain cachet in contemporary society, with the worldliness they seem to acquire from their travels and the envy-inducing social-media posts they leave in their wake. But, the researchers warn, "Whilst aspects of glamorization in regard to mobility are omnipresent in our lives, there exists an ominous silence with regard to its darker side."

The study, which synthesizes existing research on the effects of frequent travel, finds three types of consequence: physiological, psychological and emotional, and social. The physiological ones are the most obvious. Jet lag is the affliction travelers know best, although they may not anticipate some of its direr, if rarer, potential effects, like speeding ageing or increasing the risk of heart attack and stroke. Then there's the danger of deep-vein thrombosis, exposure to germs and radiation—people who fly more than 85,000 miles a year (say, New York to Seattle and back every three weeks, or New York to Tokyo and back seven times) exceed the regulatory limit for exposure to radiation.

And finally, of course, business travelers tend to get less exercise and eat less healthily than people who stay in place. The psychological and emotional toll of business travel is more abstract, but just as real. Frequent flyers experience "travel disorientation" from changing places and time zones so often. They also suffer mounting stress, given that "time spent travelling will rarely be offset through a reduced workload, and that there may be anxieties associated with work continuing to accumulate (e.g. 'inbox overload') whilst away." Due to the absence from family and friends, "hypermobility is frequently an isolating and lonely experience," the authors write.

The accumulated impact can be substantial. One study of 10,000 World Bank employees found that the business travelers among them were three times as likely to file psychological insurance claims. Finally, there are the social effects. Marriages suffer from the time apart, as does children's behavior. What is more, relationships tend to become more unequal, as the partner who stays at home is forced to take on more domestic duties. There's a gender disparity here, since most business travelers are men. Friendships also fray, as business travelers often "sacrifice local collective activities and instead priorities their immediate families when returning from trips."

Of course, these impacts are mitigated by the fact that they fall disproportionately on a segment of the population that is already doing rather well. The "mobile elite" tend to have higher incomes and access to better health care than the population at large. According to the study, in Sweden, 3% of the population accounts for a quarter of international travel; in France, 5% covers half of the population's total distance travelled. So, these may be problems of the 1% (or the 3%, or the 5%). But they're real enough regardless. By all means feel jealous of acquaintances' Instagram photos of exotic meals and faraway attractions. But harbor a small amount of concern as well.

20. Which of the following best concludes the passage?

a. There are various negative consequences of hyper-mobility, hence one should try to avoid frequent travelling.

b. Since the percentage of "mobile-elite" is so low, their problems have not been completely highlighted by media.

c. The charm of frequent traveling has been so prominent in our society that people hardly know the issues faced by this small percentage of "mobile-elite."

d. Frequent long-distance travelers tend to have much more social and psychological problems as compared to people who are settled at one place.

21. Which of the following problems is NOT linked with hyper-mobility in the passage?

a. Loneliness

b. Relationship issues

c. Social effects

d. Mortification

22. Which of the following medical conditions are frequent long-distance travelers more likely to get?

a. Height phobia

b. Cardiovascular diseases

c. Schizophrenia

d. Diabetes

23. Why does society envy frequent travelers?

    a. Frequent travelers tend to visit attractive locations and enjoy exotic meals.

    b. Hyper-mobile elite possess a cachet in the society.

    c. Less awareness exists concerning the problems faced by hyper-mobile people.

    d. All of the above.

Questions 24 - 28 refer to the following passage.

Generosity

Source: [By Terri Yablonsky, originally published on Republican-American, September 2015]

Countless studies have found that generosity, both volunteering and charitable donations, benefits young and old physically and psychologically. "Volunteering moves people into the present and distracts the mind from the stresses and problems of the self," said Stephen G. Post, founding director of the Center for Medical Humanities. "Many studies show that one of the best ways to deal with the hardships in life is not to just center on yourself but to take the opportunity to engage in simple acts of kindness." Studies show that when people think about helping others, they activate a part of the brain called the mesolimbic pathway, which is responsible for feelings of gratification.

Helping others doles out happiness chemicals, including dopamine, endorphins that block pain signals and oxytocin, known as the tranquility hormone. Even just the thought of giving money to a specific charity has this effect on the brain, research shows. Intuition tells us that giving more to oneself is the best way to be happy. But that's not the case, according to Dan Ariely, professor of behavioral economics and psychology at Duke University. "If you are a recipient of a good deed, you may have momentary happiness, but your long-term happiness is higher if you are the giver," Ariely said. For example, if you give people a gift card for a Starbucks cappuccino and call them that evening and ask how happy they are, people say they are not happier than if you hadn't given it to them. If you give another group a gift card and ask them to give it to a random person, when you call them at night, those people are happier. "People are happier when they give, even if they're just following instructions," Ariely said. "They take credit for the giving and therefore are happier at the end of the day." The way we give is important, too, Ariely said.

Taxes are a form of giving that typically does not make Americans happy. "If you give directly from a paycheck, we don't pay attention to it," he said. "It's the way we give and how we give that makes us happy. The key is to give deliberately and thoughtfully, so that other people benefit from it." Research supports this, and researchers started from a baseline of equal physical characteristics among study participants, so it wasn't a case of healthier people being more willing to volunteer.

24. Which of the following statements is NOT true according to the passage?

    a. People feel happy even if they have to be generous just to follow instructions.

    b. Charity benefits young and old physically and psychologically.

    c. One feels long-term happiness of higher level, if he/she is a recipient of good deed.

    d. The way we give and how we give is equally important to be happy.

25. Thinking of helping others activates the "Mesolimbic pathway" area of the brain. Which of the following best describes the feelings generated by this activity?

    a. Meagre

    b. Restraint

    c. Aversion

    d. Fulfilment

26. Which of the following can be safely inferred from the passage regarding intuitions?

    a. Intuitions are always correct

    b. Intuitions are always wrong

    c. Intuitions are not always correct

    d. None of the above

27. According to the research, which of the following actions would make one feel most happy and gratified?

    a. Paying of pending dues and taxes

    b. Giving beneficial gifts to others

    c. Receiving surprise gift packs

    d. Buying something which is needed urgently

28. Which of the following statements is TRUE according to the research shared in the passage?

    a. Healthier people are usually more willing to volunteer as compared to physically weak people.

    b. Acts of kindness can help a person to face the hardships of life.

    c. Helping others generate positive biological and chemical changes in our body.

    d. Both b & c

Questions 29 - 30 refer to the following passage.

Scottish Wind Farms II

There is still a public debate concerning the use of wind farms to generate energy. The most cited argument against wind energy is that the up-front investment is expensive. They also argue that it is aesthetically displeasing, they are noisy, and they create a serious threat to wildlife in the area.

While wind energy is renewable, or cannot be depleted, it does not mean that wind is always available. Wind is fluctuating, or intermittent, and therefore not suited to meet the base amount of energy demand, meaning if there is no wind then no energy is being created.

29. What is the biggest argument against wind energy?

    a. The turbines are noisy

    b. The turbines endanger wildlife

    c. The turbines are expensive to build

    d. They are aesthetically displeasing

30. What is the best way to describe this article's description of wind energy?

    a. Loud and ever present

    b. The cheapest form of renewable energy

    c. The only source of renewable energy in Scotland

    d. Clean and renewable but fluctuating

MATHEMATICS

1. 389 + 454 =

    a. 853
    b. 833
    c. 843
    d. 863

2. 9,177 + 7,204 =

    a. 16,4712
    b. 16,371
    c. 16,381
    d. 15,412

3. 2,199 + 5,832 =

    a. 8,331
    b. 8,041
    c. 8,141
    d. 8,031

4. 8,390 - 5,239 =

    a. 3,261
    b. 3,151
    c. 3,161
    d. 3,101

5. 643 - 587 =

    a. 56
    b. 66
    c. 46
    d. 55

6. 3,406 - 2,767 =

    a. 629
    b. 720
    c. 639
    d. 649

7. 149 × 7 =

    a. 1032
    b. 1043
    c. 1059
    d. 1063

8. 467 × 41 =

    a. 19,147
    b. 21,227
    c. 23,107
    d. 18,177

9. 309 × 17 =

    a. 5,303
    b. 4,913
    c. 4,773
    d. 5,253

10. 491 ÷ 9 =

    a. 54 r5
    b. 56 r6
    c. 57 r5
    d. 51 r

11. 15 is what percent of 200?

    a. 7.5%
    b. 15%
    c. 20%
    d. 17.50%

12. A boy has 5 red balls, 3 white balls and 2 yellow balls. What percent of the balls are yellow?

    a. 2%
    b. 8%
    c. 20%
    d. 12%

13. Add 10% of 300 to 50% of 20

    a. 50%
    b. 40%
    c. 60%
    d. 45%

14. Convert 75% to a fraction.

    a. 2/100
    b. 75/100
    c. 3/4
    d. 4/7

15. Convert 90% to a fraction

    a. 1/10
    b. 9/9
    c. 10/100
    d. 9/10

16. Multiply 3 by 25% of 40

   a. 75
   b. 30
   c. 68
   d. 35

17. What is 10% of 30 multiplied by 75% of 200?

   a. 450
   b. 750
   c. 20
   d. 45

18. Convert 0.28 to a fraction.

   a. 7/25
   b. 3.25
   c. 8/25
   d. 5/28

19. Convert 0.45 to a fraction

   a. 7/20
   b. 7/45
   c. 9/20
   d. 3/20

20. Convert 1/5 to percent.

   a. 10%
   b. 5%
   c. 20%
   d. 25%

21. Convert 4/20 to percent

   a. 25%
   b. 20%
   c. 40%
   d. 30%

22. Convert 0.55 to percent

   a. 45%
   b. 15%
   c. 75%
   d. 55%

23. Convert 0.33 to percent

   a. 77%
   b. 67%
   c. 33%
   d. 57%

24. A man buys an item for $420 and has a balance of $3000.00. How much did he have before?

   a. $2,580
   b. $3,420
   c. $2,420
   d. $342

25. Divide 9.60 by 3.2

   a. 2.50
   b. 3
   c. 2.3
   d. 6.4

26. What is the best approximate solution for 1.135 - 113.5?

    a. -110
    b. 100
    c. -90
    d. 110

27. If X = 7 solve $3x + 5 - 2x$

    a. x = 6
    b. x = 12
    c. x = 1
    d. x = 0

28. Solve the following equation $3(2x - 2) = 24 - 3x$

    a. x = 24
    b. x = 9
    c. x = 10
    d. x = 3.33

29. Solve $3x - 27 = 0$

    a. x = 24
    b. x = 30
    c. x = 9
    d. x = 21

30. Solve the following equation 4(y + 6) = 3y + 30

   a. y = 6
   b. y = 20
   c. y = 30/7
   d. y = 30

MECHANICAL COMPREHENSION

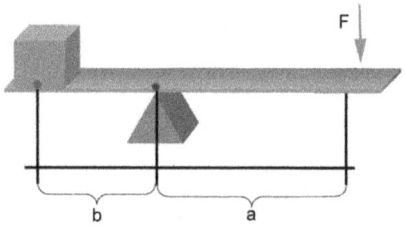

1. Consider the illustration above and the corresponding data:

Weight = W = 200 pounds
Distance from fulcrum to Weight = b = 10 feet
Distance from fulcrum to point where force is applied = a = 20 feet
How much force (F) must be applied to lift the weight?

   a. 80
   b. 100
   c. 150
   d. 200

2. A force of 20 kg. is applied to two springs in series, which compresses the springs 6 inches. If the same force is applied to springs in parallel, how far will the springs compress?

   a. 6 inches
   b. 3 inches
   c. 2 inches
   d. 1 inch

3. You are asked to determine the gear ratio of a vehicle. You open the differential and observe the ring gear the and pinion gear. The ring gear has 40 teeth and the pinion gear has 8, What is the gear ratio of the vehicle?

    a. 4:1
    b. 5:1
    c. 8:2
    d. 8:0

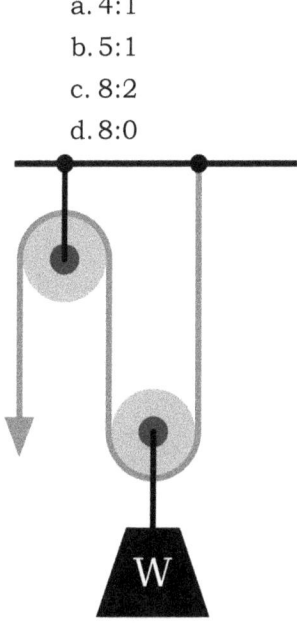

4. Consider the pulley arrangement above. If the weight, W, is 50 pounds, how much force is required to lift it?

    a. 10 pounds
    b. 20 pounds
    c. 25 pounds
    d. 50 pounds

5. Consider a gear train with 3 gears, from left to right, A with 20 teeth, gear B with 60 teeth, and gear C with 10 teeth. Gear A turns clockwise at 60 rpm. What direction and speed in rpm does Gear C turn?

   a. 120 rpm, clockwise
   b. 100 rpm clockwise
   c. 120 rpm counter clockwise
   d. 140 rpm counter clockwise

6. If a 100-pound object is sitting on a 10-square-inch plate, what is the PSI?

   a. 5
   b. 10
   c. 15
   d. 20

7.

8.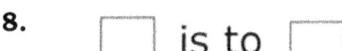

a. ⌒   b. ◠

c. ⌃   d. ⊔

9.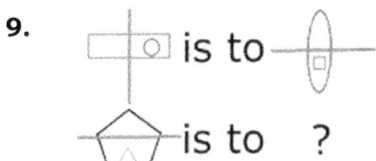

a. ⬡   b. △

c. ▭   d. ⊕

10.

a. ●   b. ▭

c. ⬢   d. ⌒

11. Find the weight of the load L in N, if the pulling force F=20 N.

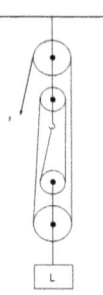

12. How many blocks is the block A in the figure touching?

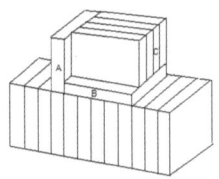

a. 4
b. 5
c. 6
d. 7

13. Which shape must we place on the existing figure to form a perfect square?

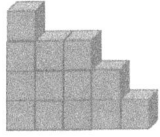

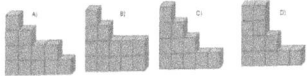

14. How many cubes must we add in the figure to form a perfect cube?

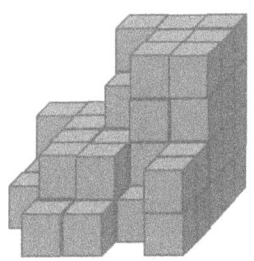

a. 55
b. 45
c. 70
d. 125

+15. Which shape must we place on the existing figure to form a perfect cube?

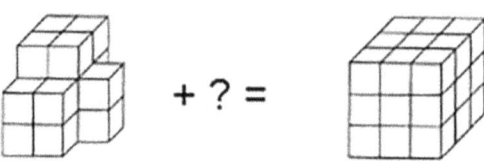

a. b.

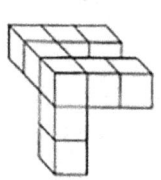   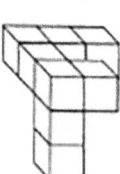

c. d.

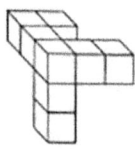   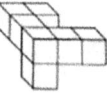

16. Which figure can you form with the following pieces?

a. b. c. d.

17. Which figure can you form with the following pieces?

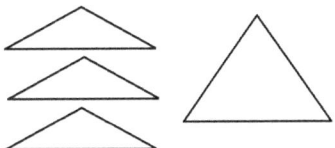

a. 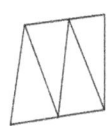 b. 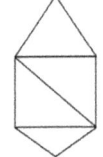 c. 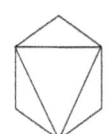 d.

18. What is the minimum force (in N) needed to lift the 600 N object, if x = 3 m and y = 2 m?

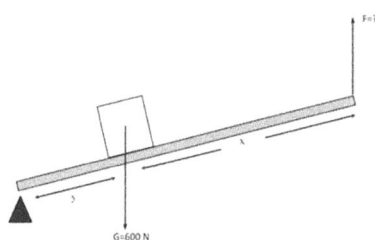

a. 400
b. 320
c. 240
d. 180

154   PRACTICE THE EIAT!

19. What is the distance between the mass m and the fulcrum, if the system is in equilibrium and the length of the rod d is 120 cm? Give the answer in cm.

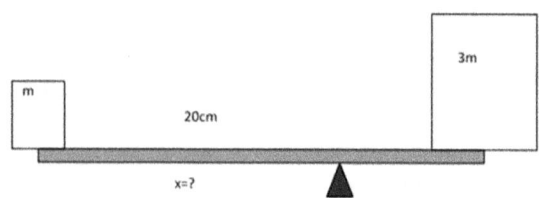

a. 80
b. 85
c. 90
d. 95

20. Which figure represents the assembly of the following pieces?

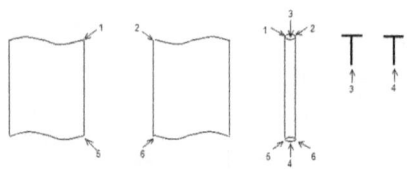

a.   b.   c.   d.

21. Which figure represents the assembly of the following pieces?

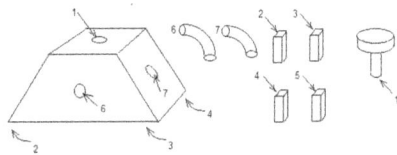

a.   b.   c.   d.

22. How many blocks is the block B in the figure touching?

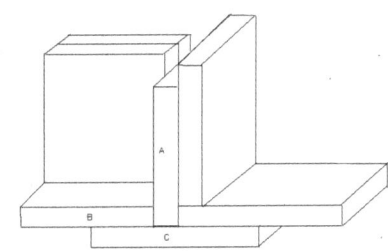

    a. 4
    b. 5
    c. 6
    d. 3

23. Which shape must we place on the figure below to form a perfect cube?

a.   b.   c.   d.

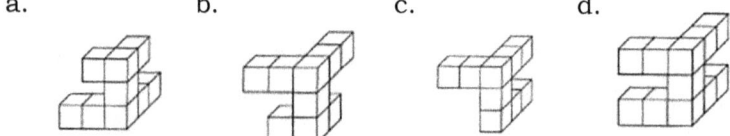

24. Which figure can you form with the following pieces?

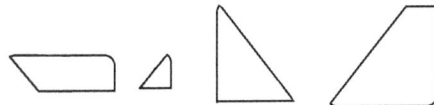

a.

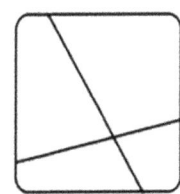

b.

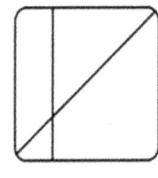

c.

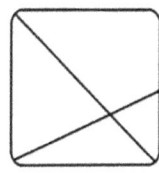

d.

25. What is the value of the force F enough to lift the object up, if the weight W of the object is 360 N?

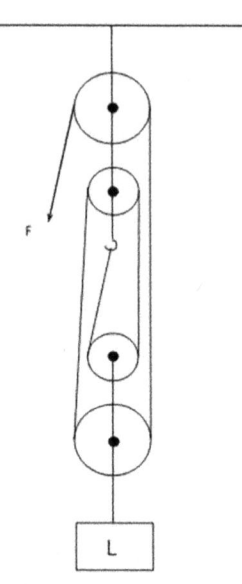

a. 180 N
b. 120 N
c. 90 N
d. 72 N

26. Find the value of the ratio F/W, if R/r = 3.

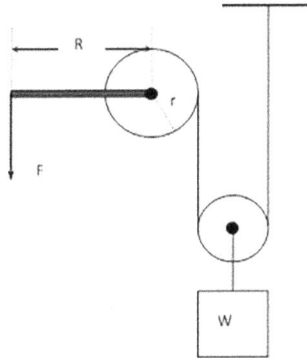

a. 3
b. 1/3
c. 6
d. 1/6

27. Which of the following are effects of electricity?

I. Lighting
II. Physical
III. Magnetic
IV. Lifting

    a. I,II,III
    b. I,III
    c. II,IV
    d. II,III,IV

28. What direction does the rack in the figure move if the pinion rotates clockwise?

a. Left
b. Right
c. Up
d. Down

29. If the weight of the homogeneous rod is 10 N, what must be the load on the other end of the rod be to balance it?

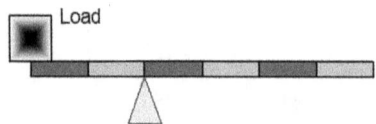

a. 5 N
b. 10 N
c. 20 N
d. 40 N

30. Which type of lever does the wheel and axle system shown represent?

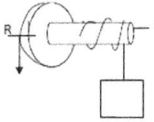

a. First class lever
b. Second class lever
c. Third class lever
d. Fourth class lever

Answer Key

1. A
We know that an annex is like an attic because the text states the annex was above Otto Frank's building.

Choice B is incorrect because an office building doesn't have bedrooms. Choice C is incorrect because a basement would be below the office building. Choice D is incorrect because there would not be a kitchen in an office building.

2. B
The diary has been published in 55 languages so people all over the world can learn about Anne. That is why the passage says it has been continuously in print.

Choice A is incorrect because it is too vague. Choice C is incorrect because it was published after Anne died and she did not write in all three languages. Choice D is incorrect because the passage does not give us any information about what languages Otto Frank spoke.

3. C
Use the process of elimination to figure this out.

Choice A cannot be the correct answer because, otherwise the passage would have simply said that Anne and Margot both died of starvation. Choices B and D cannot be correct because, if the Germans had done something specifically to murder Anne, the passage would have stated that directly. By the process of elimination, choice C has to be the correct answer.

4. D
We can figure this out using context clues. The paragraph is talking about Anne's diary and so, outlet in this instance is a place where Anne can pour her feelings.

Choice A is incorrect answer. That is the literal meaning of the word outlet and the passage is using the figurative meaning. Choice B is incorrect because that is the secondary literal meaning of the word outlet, as in an outlet mall. Again, we are looking for figurative meaning. Choice C is incorrect because

there are no clues in the text to support that answer.
5. B
When someone is avid about something that means they are highly interested in the subject. The context clues are dull and boring, because they define the opposite of avid.

6. A
The author is using a simile to compare the books to medicine. Medicine is what you take when you want to feel better. They are suggesting that if you want to feel good, they should read Dr. Seuss' books.

Choice B is incorrect because there is no mention of a doctor's office. Choice C is incorrect because it is using the literal meaning of medicine and the author is using medicine in a figurative way. Choice D is incorrect because it makes no sense. We know not to eat books.

7. D
The publisher is described as intelligent because he knew to get in touch with a famous author to develop a book that children would be interested in reading.

Choice A is incorrect because we can assume that all book publishers must know how to read. Choice B is incorrect because it says in the article that more than one publisher was concerned whether children liked to read. Choice D is incorrect because there is no mention in the article about how well The Cat in the Hat sold when it was first published.

8. B
The passage describes in detail how Dr. Seuss had a great effect on the lives of children through his writing. It names several of his books, tells how he helped children become avid readers and explains his style of writing.

Choice A is incorrect because that is just one single fact about the passage. Choice C is incorrect because that is just one single fact about the passage. Choice D is incorrect because that is just one single fact about the passage. Again, choice B is correct because it encompasses ALL the facts in the passage, not just one single fact.

9. B
The general tone is informal.

10. B
The statement, "Fewer people have aquariums in their office than at home," cannot be inferred from this article.

11. C
The author does not provide evidence for this statement.

12. B
The following statement is an opinion, " Aquarium gravel improves the aesthetics of the aquarium."

13. A
Secede means to break away from because the 11 states wanted to leave the United States and form their own country.

Choice B is incorrect because the states were not accomplishing anything. Choice C is incorrect because the states were trying to leave the USA not join it. Choice D is incorrect because the states seceded before they lost the war.

14. B
Look at the dates in the passage. The shots were fired on April 12 and Congress declared war on April 14.

Choice C is incorrect because the passage states that Lincoln was against slavery. Choice D is incorrect because it never mentions who was or was not at Fort Sumter.

15. C
The passage states that Lee surrendered to Grant after the capture of the capital of the Confederacy, which is Richmond.

Choice A is incorrect because the war continued for 2 years after Gettysburg. Choice B is incorrect because that battle is not mentioned in the passage. Choice D is incorrect because the capture of the capital occurred after the march to the sea.

16. C
Choice A is incorrect because it cannot be directly inferred from the passage, Choices B and D are implied in the passage

but do not summarize the complete message conveyed in the passage. Choice C best summarizes the study and facts in the passage.

17. D
"Digital sunset" has been related to logging out of all online/social media applications and putting cell phones away. Choice D is the correct answer.

18. C
Choices A, B and D are directly mentioned in the passage. However, Choice C has not been discussed as it is. Depression, anxiety and schizophrenia have been linked to excessive use of social media by youth, and deficiency of sleep has been stated due to online presence at night. However, these have not been directly linked to deficiency of sleep in the passage.

19. B
Adolescents are young people going through the process of developing from a child into an adult. Choices C and D are incorrect. Choice A is too a generic category. Choice C (Pubescent is the synonym) is the correct answer.

20. D
Choice A is incorrect since the passage does not suggest avoiding frequent travel. Choices B and D do not directly conclude the passage. Hence, Choice C is the correct answer which clearly concludes the message being conveyed in the passage.

21. D
Choices A, B and C have all been linked to frequent traveling in the passage. Mortification indicates humiliation which is not faced by hyper-mobile people.

22. B
As per passage, one of the physiological issues associated with frequent long-distance travelers is "Jet-Lag", which increases the risk of heart attack and stroke. Hence choice B is the correct choice. Choices A, C and D are incorrect as these are not related to traveling.

23. D
All choices, A, B and C are implied in the passage. The general public fantasizes about frequent travelling and being hyper-mobile due to tourism opportunities, exotic meals and lack of knowledge about the "darker side" of being hyper-mobile.

24. C
Choices A, B and D have been discussed in the passage to be true. Choice C is a false statement since one feels long-term happiness of a higher level if he/she is a giver not the recipient. Hence choice C is the correct answer.

25. D
Studies show that when people think about helping others, they activate a part of the brain called the mesolimbic pathway, which is responsible for feelings of "gratification". The best synonym for gratification is Choice D, fulfillment.

26. C
According to the passage: Intuition tells us that giving more to oneself is the best way to be happy but it's NOT the actual case. Study revealed that people get happier while giving away to others. Hence intuition is incorrect in this case and thus choice A is not the correct answer. Having said this, one case is not enough to infer that all intuitions are incorrect, so choice B is also incorrect. Choice C, is the safest to infer from this scenario which suggests that intuitions may or may not be correct.

27. B
Study suggests that true happiness is achieved when one gives others rather than receiving. Choice C and C are incorrect. Choice A is incorrect since it has been discussed in the passage that paying bills and taxes is a type of giving, which does not usually make people happy. Choice B is the correct answer.

28. D
Choice A is incorrect since the study concluded that results were independent of physical characteristics. Choices B and C are discussed in the passage as true statements.

29. C
The upfront cost is expensive.
The other choices may appear to be correct, and even be common sense, but they are not specifically mentioned in the paragraph.

30. D
The best way to describe the paragraphs description of wind energy is clean and renewable but fluctuating.
The other choices are good descriptions of wind energy, but not the best way to describe the article.

Mathematics

1. C
389 + 454 = 843

2. C
9,177 + 7,204 = 16,381

3. D
2,199 + 5,832 = 8,031

4. B
8,390 - 5,239 = 3,151

5. A
643 - 587 = 56

6. C
3,406 - 2,767 = 639

7. B
149 × 7 = 1043

8. A
467 × 41 = 19,147

9. D
309 × 17 = 52,53

10. A
491 ÷ 9 = 54 r5

11. A
15% = 15/100 X 200 = 7.5%

12. C
Total no. of balls = 10, no. of yellow balls = 2. 2/10 X 100 = 20%

13. B
10% of 300 = 30 and 50% of 20 = 10 so 30 + 10 = 40.

14. C
75%= 75/100 = ¾

15. D
90% = 90/100 = 9/10

16. B
25% of 40 = 10 and 10 x 3 = 30

17. A
10% of 30 = 3 and 75% of 200 = 150, 3 X 150 = 450

18. A
0.28 = 28/100 = 7/25

19. C
0.45 = 45/100 = 9/20

20. C
1/5 X 100 = 20%

21. B
4/20 X 100 = 1/5 X 100 = 20%

22. D
0.55 X 100 = 55%

23. C
0.33 X 100 = 33%

24. B
(Amount Spent) $420 + $3000 (Balance) = $3420

25. B
9.60 / 3.2 = 3

26. A
1.135 -113.5 = 1.135 -113.5 = -112.37. Best approximate = -110

27. B
X=7, so 3x = 3 x 7 = 21, 2x = 2 x 7 = 14, so 21 + 5 - 14 = 26 - 14 = 12

28. D
6x – 6 = 24 – 3x, = 6x + 3x -6 = 24, = 9x – 6 = 24, = 9x = 24 + 6, = 9x = 30, = x = 30/9, = x = 3.33

29. C
3x = 27, x = 27/3, x = 9
4. B 4y + 6 = 3y + 30, = 4y – 3y + 6 = 30, = y + 6 = 30, = y = 30 – 6, = y = 24

30. A
4y + 24 = 3y + 30, = 4y – 3y + 24 = 30, = y + 24 = 30, = y = 30 – 24, = y = 6

Mechanical Comprehension

1. B
To solve for F, Weight X b (distance from fulcrum to weight) = Force X a (distance from fulcrum to point where force is applied)
200 X 10 = F X 20
2000/20 = F
F = 100

2. B
If the springs in series compress 6 inches, then the springs in parallel will compress half that amount, or 3 inches.

3. B
Opening the differential, the ring gear is the larger gear and the pinion the smaller. The gear differential is calculated by

dividing the number of teeth on the pinion into the number of teeth on the ring gear. 40/8 = 5, or 5:1.

4. C
Since the weight is only attached to one pulley, the force required will be 50/2 = 25 pounds.

5. A
First calculate the speed of gear B. The gear ratio is 60:20 or 3:1. If gear A is turning at 60 rpm, then gear B will turn at 30/3 = 20 rpm.

Next calculate B and C. Gear C is smaller, so it will turn faster. The gear ratio is 60:10 or 6:1, and since gear B turns at 20 rpm, gear C will turn at 20 X 6 = 120 rpm.

Next calculate the direction. Gear A is turning clockwise, so Gear B is turning counter clockwise, so Gear C must be turning clockwise.

6. B
Calculate the PSI by taking the weight divided by the size of the object the weight is bearing on. 100/10 = 10 PSI.

7. D
The relationship is the same figure flipped vertically, so the best choice is D.

8. C
The relation is the same figure with the bottom half removed.

9. D
The first pair is a rectangle with a circle inside and then an oval with a square inside. The given figures in the second pair has a triangle inside, so the match will be the circle with a square inside.

10. B
The relation is two upright figures in the first set, and 2 horizontal figures in the second set.

11. D
The block and tackle system composed by a system of pulleys as shown operates according the following rule:

Pulling Force=Load/(Number of supporting ropes)
Here, the number of supporting ropes is 4. So, we have
20 = Load/4
So, Load = 20 × 4 = 80 N.

Do not confuse the number of supporting ropes. The rope, which is being pulled is not counted. Otherwise, you will obtain the wrong answer, Choice B 100 (20 × 5).

12. C
From the figure, block A touches 6 blocks (1 is below, 4 are lateral in vertical position and 1 is lateral in the horizontal position.

13. A
The figure has 4 rows and 5 columns, with not all of them are complete. It is obvious that to be a perfect square, it must have 5 × 5 dimensions.

From the figure, you may see that the first (bottom) row is complete. In the second row one cube is missing, in the third row two cubes are missing, in the fourth row four cubes are missing and in the fifth row all 5 cubes are missing. There missing cubes must be filled with one of the shapes.

14. C
There are 5 cubes in the longest row, we need 5 × 5 × 5 = 125 cubes in total to form a perfect cube.

First, count the existing cubes. In the first row, there are 5 + 4 + 5 + 5 + 4 = 23 cubes.

In the second row, there are 5 + 3 + 4 + 4 + 1 = 17 cubes.
In the third row, there are 3 + 3 + 2 = 8 cubes.
In the fourth row, there are 3 + 3 + 1 = 7 cubes.

Total cubes, 23 + 17 + 8 + 7 = 55 cubes.
To calculate the total number to form a perfect cube, 125 – 55 = 70 cubes.

15. A
If you rotate the shapes in the choices by 900 clockwise, you will notice that the missing shape to form a perfect cube is the first one.

16. B
Since the pieces are identical, choices C and D can be eliminated right away. Consider only choices A and B for the correct answer. Choice A shows a square divided into four, and clearly the figures given are larger than one-quarter. Choice B is the only choice that fits the description.

17. C
There are three identical right triangles and one equilateral triangle in the separate pieces. Choices A, B, and D can be eliminated, leaving only choice C, which contains an equilateral triangle.

18. C
This is a second-class lever as the Load is between pivot and force.
The equation of levers is
Load × Load distance = Force × Force distance
Here, Load = G = 600N, Load distance = y = 2m, Force distance = x + y = 3m + 2m = 5m and calculate the force.
So,
600 X 2 = F X 5
F = (600 X 2)/5 = 1200/5 = 240N

19. C
This is an example of first-class lever as the pivot (fulcrum) is between Load and Force.
The equation of levers is
Load × Load distance = Force × Force distance
Here, Load = 3m · g, Force = m · g, Load distance = (120 – x) cm, and Force distance = x cm. Here, we have to calculate the force distance. So,
3mg × (120 - x) = mg × x
Simplifying mg from both sides, the equation becomes,
3 × (120 - x) = x
3 × 120 – 3 × x = x
4x = 360
X = 90c

20. D
If two pieces have the same number at the position shown, it means that point is a junction point. Here, the rod connects the two wide wavy pieces and the two T-shapes are at the edges of the central rod.

21. B
If two pieces have the same number at the position shown, it means that point is a junction point. Here, the hoses are at the central holes of the lateral faces of the platform, the screw-like shape is on top of the platform and the small cuboids act as legs.

22. A
From the figure, block B touches 1 block below, 2 blocks above and one block laterally, i.e. in total 4 blocks.

23. D
There are 5 missing cubes in the first (bottom) row, 1 in the second and 5 in the third row. The only shape that fits the description is the fourth one. No rotation needed here.

24. B
There are two quadrilaterals and two triangles in the original figure. Choice A contains four quadrilaterals, so it is not the right shape and can be eliminated. You can also eliminate choice C, which contains one quadrilateral and three triangles, and choice D, which contains three quadrilaterals and one triangle.

This leaves only choice B, which contains two quadrilaterals and two triangles.

25. C
The block and tackle system composed by a system of pulleys as shown operates according the following rule:

Pulling Force=Load/(Number of supporting ropes)
Here Load and Weight are the same thing.
Here, the number of supporting ropes is 4. So, we have
F = 360/4

Force = 90 N Choice C

Feedback for Choice D - Do not confuse the number of supporting ropes. The rope which is being pulled, is not counted. Otherwise, you will obtain the wrong answer Choice D 72 (360 / 5).

26. D
Here it is a combined system of simple machines composed by a Wheel and Axle and a Movable pulley system.
For the wheel and axle, the mechanical advantage is
MA1 = R / r. Here, MA1 = 3.

For movable pulleys, the mechanical advantage MA2 is 2. So, the combined mechanical advantage is MAtotal = MA1 × MA2 = 3 × 2 = 6.

This means the force needed to lift the load is 6 time smaller than the load itself. So, F/W = 1/6

27. D
"Physical" is not an effect of electricity. The other 3 are related to electricity. Lighting effect of electricity is observed when you turn on a lamp. Magnetism is an effect of electricity observed in electromagnets. Lifting is an effect of electricity observed in cranes.

28. A
If the pinion rotates clockwise, its lower teeth move due left. Therefore, the rack shifts left as well.

29. A
If we use a force in the right side of the bar, the equation becomes, an example of a first class lever in which pivot is located between Load and Force.

The equation of levers is
Load ×Load distance=Force ×Force distance

Here, Load = 10N, Force is unknown, Load distance = 2 units, and Force distance = 4 units. Thus,

10N × 2units = F × 4 units
F = (10N × 2 units) / 4 units
F = 5N

30. A

A lateral view of the Wheel and Axle system is shown on the right. The pivot is at the common center of the two circles. Force is on the left side and Load is on the right one. Therefore, this is an example of first class lever (Force – Pivot – Load).

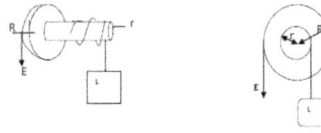

CONCLUSION

CONGRATULATIONS! You have made it this far because you have applied yourself diligently to practicing for the exam and no doubt improved your potential score considerably! Getting into a good school is a huge step in a journey that might be challenging at times but will be many times more rewarding and fulfilling. That is why being prepared is so important.

Study then Practice and then Succeed!

Good Luck!

THANKS!

VISIT US ONLINE

www.test-preparation.ca

www.ingramcontent.com/pod-product-compliance
Lightning Source LLC
LaVergne TN
LVHW010259260326
834688LV00044B/1372